Assessment

Bothell, WA • Chicago, IL • Columbus, OH • New York, NY

Assessment

Cover: Nathan Love

mheducation.com/prek-12

Send all inquiries to:
McGraw-Hill Education
Two Penn Plaza
New York, New York 10121

ISBN: 978-0-02-129750-4
MHID: 0-02-129750-9

Printed in the United States of America.

6 7 8 9 10 11 QVS 20 19 18 17 16

B

TABLE OF CONTENTS

Weekly Assessment

Mid-Unit Assessment

Unit Assessment

Exit Assessment

TABLE OF CONTENTS

Oral Reading Fluency Assessment

Scoring Sheets

Answer Keys

Assessment

The *Assessment* BLM is an integral part of the complete assessment program aligned with the core reading and intervention curriculums of *McGraw-Hill Reading WonderWorks* and *McGraw-Hill Reading Wonders.*

Purpose of *Assessment*

The instruction in *McGraw-Hill Reading WonderWorks* is parallel to the instruction in *McGraw-Hill Reading Wonders*. Student results in *Assessment* provide a picture of achievement within *McGraw-Hill Reading WonderWorks* and a signal as to whether students can successfully transition back to Approaching Level reading instruction.

Assessment offers the opportunity to monitor student progress in a steady and structured manner while providing formative assessment data.

As students complete each week of the intervention program, they will be assessed on their understanding of weekly vocabulary words and their ability to access and comprehend complex literary and informational selections using text evidence.

At the key 3-week and 6-week reporting junctures, assessments measure student understanding of previously-taught vocabulary words and comprehension skills and provide evidence of student progress through the curriculum. If students show a level of mastery at the end of a unit, an assessment to exit out of *McGraw-Hill Reading WonderWorks* and into the Approaching Level instruction of *McGraw-Hill Reading Wonders* is available.

Throughout the unit, oral reading fluency passages are available to measure student ability to read connected text fluently, accurately, and with a measure of prosody.

The results of the assessments provided in *Assessment* can be used to inform subsequent instruction and assist with grouping and leveling designations.

Components of *Assessment*

- Weekly Assessment
- Mid-Unit Assessment
- Unit Assessment
- Exit Assessment
- Oral Reading Fluency Assessment

Assessment focuses on key areas of English Language Arts—Reading, Language, and Fluency. To assess Reading and Language proficiency, students read selections and respond to items focusing on comprehension skills, vocabulary words, literary elements, and text features. These items assess the ability to access meaning from the text and demonstrate understanding of words and phrases. To assess Fluency, students read passages for one minute to measure their words correct per minute (WCPM) and accuracy rates.

Weekly Assessment

The Weekly Assessment features a "cold read" reading selection (informational or narrative based on the weekly reading focus) and 5 items—three items on the weekly comprehension skill and two items that ask students to show how context helps them identify the meaning of a vocabulary word. (For weeks in which poetry is the featured genre, vocabulary items are replaced by items assessing literary elements.) Students will provide text evidence to support their answers.

Administering Weekly Assessment

Each test should be administered once the instruction for the specific week is completed. Make a copy of the assessment and the Scoring Sheet for each student. The Scoring Sheet allows for informal comments on student responses and adds to an understanding of strengths and weaknesses.

After each student has a copy of the assessment, provide a version of the following directions: Say: *Write your name and the date on the question pages for this assessment.* (When students are finished, continue with the directions.) *You will read a selection and answer questions about it. Read the selection and the questions that follow it carefully. Write your responses on the lines provided. Go back to the text to underline and circle the text evidence that supports your answers. When you have completed the assessment, put your pencil down and turn the pages over. You may begin now.*

Answer procedural questions during the assessment, but do not provide any assistance on the items or selections. After the class has completed the assessment, ask students to verify that their names and the date are written on the necessary pages.

Alternatively, you may choose to work through the assessment with the students. This will provide an additional opportunity for you to observe their ability to access complex text in a more informal group setting.

Evaluating the Weekly Assessment

Each Weekly Assessment is worth 10 points, with each item worth 2 points. Use the scoring rubric below to assign a point total per item. A Weekly Answer Key is provided to help with scoring. Student results should provide a clear picture of their understanding of the weekly comprehension skill and the weekly vocabulary words. Reteach tested skills if assessment results point to a clear deficiency.

Weekly Assessment Scoring Rubric	
Score	**Description**
2	• Reasonable, clear, and specific • Supported by accurate and relevant text evidence • Shows ability to access complex text
1	• Reasonable but somewhat unclear or vague • Supported by general, incomplete, partially accurate, or partially relevant text evidence • Shows some ability to access complex text
0	• Incorrect, unreasonable, or too vague to understand • Not supported by relevant text evidence • Shows no understanding of how to access complex text

Evidence may be specific words from the text or a paraphrase.

Assessment • Teacher Introduction

Mid-Unit Assessment

The Mid-Unit Assessment presents a snapshot of student understanding at the key 3-week instructional interval. This test features two "cold read" reading selections and 10 selected response items—seven items on the featured comprehension skills in Weeks 1–3 and three items that ask students to show how context helps them identify the meaning of a vocabulary word.

Administering Mid-Unit Assessment

Each test should be administered at the end of Week 3 instruction. Make a copy of the assessment and the Scoring Sheet for each student.

After each student has a copy of the assessment, provide a version of the following directions: Say: *Write your name and the date on the question pages for this assessment.* (When students are finished, continue with the directions.) *You will read two selections and answer questions about them. Read the selections and the questions that follow them carefully. Choose the correct answer to each question and completely fill in the bubble next to it. When you have completed the assessment, put your pencil down and turn the pages over. You may begin now.*

NOTE: The directions above can be used when students take the Unit and Exit Assessments.

Evaluating the Mid-Unit Assessment

Each Mid-Unit Assessment is worth 10 points, with each item worth 1 point. An Answer Key is provided to help with scoring. Note student success or difficulty with specific skills. Use this data to determine the instructional focus going forward. Reteach tested skills for students who score 5 points or less on the comprehension items and 2 points or less on the vocabulary items.

Unit and Exit Assessment

The Unit Assessment tests student mastery of the key instructional content featured in the unit. This test features two "cold read" reading selections (one narrative text and one informational text) and 15 selected response items—ten items on the unit's comprehension skills and five items that ask students to show how context helps them identify the meaning of a vocabulary word.

The Exit Assessment is a "parallel" test to the Unit Assessment. It assesses the same skills and pool of vocabulary words using the same format. The key differentiator between the tests is the higher level of text complexity featured in the reading selections, a level more in line with the rigor found in Approaching Level *McGraw-Hill Reading Wonders* materials.

Moving from Unit to Exit Assessment

Administer the Unit Assessment to ALL students at the close of unit instruction. Make a copy of the assessment and the Scoring Sheet for each student. Each Unit Assessment is worth 15 points, with each item worth 1 point. An Answer Key is provided to help with scoring.

If students score 13 or higher on the Unit Assessment, administer the Exit Assessment. The Exit Assessment is ONLY for those students who reach this Unit Assessment benchmark.

Oral Reading Fluency Assessment

Fluency passages are included to help assess the level at which students have progressed beyond decoding into comprehension. When readers can read the words in connected text automatically, they are free to focus on using the critical thinking skills essential to constructing meaning from complex text.

24 fiction and nonfiction passages are included to help you assess fluency. The passages are set in three Unit/Lexile bands—the first set of eight is for Units 1 and 2, the next set of eight is for Units 3 and 4, and the final set of eight is for Units 5 and 6.

See pages 6 and 7 of *Fluency Assessment* for directions on administering and scoring oral reading fluency passages and for the unit-specific benchmark WCPM scores.

Transitioning into *McGraw-Hill Reading Wonders* Instruction

Moving students into Approaching Level *McGraw-Hill Reading Wonders* instruction at the completion of a unit should be guided by assessment data, student performance during the unit instruction, and informal observation of student progress.

Use the following assessment criteria to help judge student readiness for Approaching Level designation and materials:

• Unit Assessment score of 13 or higher

• Ability to comprehend and analyze the Level Up Approaching Leveled Reader

• Score of 4 or higher on Level Up Write About Reading assignment

• Mastery of the unit benchmark skills in the Foundational Skills Kit and PowerPAL

• WCPM score and accuracy rate that meet or exceed the unit goals

• Exit Assessment score of 13 or higher

Weekly Assessment

Read "A Little Help from Her Friends" before you answer Numbers 1 through 5.

A Little Help from Her Friends

Mom's birthday was soon. But Cam's piggy bank was empty. She had no **savings** at a real bank either.

As Cam grabbed Rudy's leash to walk him, she had a great idea. Many of her neighbors left their dogs home all day while they went to work. Maybe they would pay Cam to walk their dogs after school. After checking with her mom, she put up signs around the neighborhood.

Within a few days, Cam earned a lot of money. Soon she could **afford** to buy her mom a gift.

On Monday, she picked up the dogs for their walk. As she headed down the street, she tripped over the leashes.

Two friends saw Cam. She was sitting on the ground. "Can we help?" they asked.

Cam rubbed the painful lump on her ankle. There would be no more dog walking this week. She thought quickly. "Can you walk dogs?" she asked.

"I can help on Tuesday and Thursday," said Alice.

"I can help on Wednesday and Friday," said Clara.

Cam did some math in her head. She could pay her friends a little less than she was earning. That way, she could still save enough money for Mom's gift!

GO ON →

Name: _____ **Date:** _____

Use "A Little Help from Her Friends" to answer Numbers 1 through 5.

1 **Circle** clues that help you figure out the meaning of the word *savings*.

What does *savings* mean?

_____

2 **Underline** details that tell about Cam's great idea.

What does Cam do right after telling her mom about her idea?

_____

_____

3 **Circle** words that show why Cam will soon be able to *afford* to buy a gift.

What does *afford* mean?

_____

4 **Draw a box** around the sentence that tells what happens right before Cam's friends see her on the ground.

5 **Underline** the details that tell when Cam's friends can help walk dogs for her.

Who will help the day after Cam's fall?

_____

_____

STOP

Read "Moving to the City" before you answer Numbers 1 through 5.

Moving to the City

I live in a small town near a large city. This morning, Father said, "Samir, we must move to the city because I have a new job there."

I could not believe what I had heard. Suddenly, I felt very **anxious** and ran outside. "It will take a while to make new friends," I thought. The worst part was that I would have to leave my best friend, Ahmed. I did not want to move!

When I went back inside, Mother seemed **distracted**. I tried to talk to her about my fears, but she did not pay attention. She was busy rushing around and putting things in boxes. I stood in front of her, and she stopped to look at me.

"What is wrong?" she asked. "Why are you upset?"

"Mother, I will not know anyone in the city," I said.

"Samir, you ran outside before we could tell you the rest of our news," Mother said. Then she gave me a big smile. "Ahmed and his family also are moving to the city, and we will be neighbors."

I gave a shout of delight. Now I was not so nervous about our move. I ran to call Ahmed.

GO ON →

Name: _____ Date: _____

Use "Moving to the City" to answer Numbers 1 through 5.

1 **Underline** the details that show why Samir feels *anxious* at the beginning of the story.

Write the meaning of *anxious*.

_____

_____

2 What is Samir's problem in the story?

_____

_____

Circle the detail that tells Samir's problem.

3 How does Samir try to solve his problem?

_____

_____

_____

4 **Underline** the clues in the text that show that Samir's mother is *distracted*.

What does *distracted* mean?

_____

5 **Draw a box** around the details that show the solution to Samir's problem.

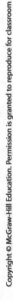

STOP

Read "An Artist of Nature" before you answer Numbers 1 through 5.

An Artist of Nature

Early Years

Young Ansel Adams played alone along the sand dunes near San Francisco. To the shy boy, the sand and waves were good company. He learned to find peace in nature here.

Adams visited Yosemite Valley with his parents. This park is in California. He took pictures of the **sheer**, steep rock walls with his camera. This is how his love for photography began.

A First Job

Later, Adams worked for the Sierra Club. This group helps people explore and protect nature. The job was at Yosemite. So, Adams spent a lot of his free time there.

Adams loved the park's rocks and trees. He studied the light and shadows. He photographed the **spectacular** scenery. Adams was always amazed by what he saw.

A Gifted Artist

The Sierra Club published Adams's photos. These photos urged people to protect nature. People in Congress saw his pictures, too. As a result, they created more national parks like Yosemite. President Carter said that because of Adams, "so much of America has been saved for future Americans." Adams's work is still remembered today.

GO ON →

Name: _____ Date: _____

Use "An Artist of Nature" to answer Numbers 1 through 5.

1 **Underline** the details that tell where Adams played when he was young.

What was an effect of the time that Adams spent playing outdoors?

_____

_____

2 **Circle** a word that means the same as *sheer*.

3 **Underline** the details in the third paragraph that tell why Adams spent so much time at Yosemite.

4 **Circle** the clues that tell how Adams felt when he looked at the *spectacular* scenery in the park.

What does *spectacular* mean?

_____

_____

5 What caused people in Congress to create more national parks?

_____

_____

Draw a box around details in the text that support your answer.

STOP

Read "Ray Kurzweil, Inventor" before you answer Numbers 1 through 5.

Ray Kurzweil, Inventor

Ray Kurzweil thinks that inventing is like surfing. He says, "you have to catch the wave at the right time." Ray catches lots of waves. Make that *brain* waves.

Ray was born in 1948. His parents were very creative. His dad was a musician. His mom was an artist.

For a science fair in the 1960s, Ray made a computer that wrote music. It won first prize worldwide. A few years later, Ray started a company that used computers to help students choose the right college.

In the 1970s, Ray sat by a blind man on a plane. The man was Stevie Wonder, a famous musician. As they talked, Ray got an idea. He made a machine that read books aloud. This machine changed people's lives, including Stevie's.

Ray and Stevie became friends. Their friendship led to another invention. Ray's new machine could make the sounds of any instrument.

Some people have compared Ray to Thomas Edison. Like Edison, Ray invented many useful **devices**. They include a scanner and a computer music keyboard.

Ray owes a lot of his success to his friends and teachers. They **enthusiastically** and eagerly supported him. Ray says, "Encouragement is necessary for young inventors to succeed."

GO ON →

Name: _____ Date: _____

Use "Ray Kurzweil, Inventor" to answer Numbers 1 through 5.

1 What key event happened in Ray's life before he started his own company?

_____

_____

Underline the details that tell when this event happened.

2 **Draw a box** around the words that tell when Ray got an idea while on a plane.

3 **Circle** the words in the text that are examples of *devices*.

Write the meaning of *devices*.

_____

_____

4 Tell what happened after Ray and Stevie became friends.

_____

_____

5 **Circle** the clues that tell the meaning of *enthusiastically*.

What does *enthusiastically* mean?

_____

_____

STOP

Read "A Better Way to Read" before you answer Numbers 1 through 5.

A Better Way to Read

You read at school and at home. But how do you read? You may read some books that are printed on paper. You may also read modern e-books. (The *e* stands for *electronic*.)

Here is a short **analysis** of some pros and cons of e-books. It is a close look at what people like and dislike about e-books.

Benefits of E-Books

E-books have great features. Suppose you do not understand a word. With some e-books, you can just touch a button to hear the word or find out what it means. Some e-books have other features, such as sound or animation.

E-books are easy to carry around. No one wants to carry heavy books, but you can store a whole stack of e-books on a digital reader. That makes backpacks much lighter and safer.

Problems with E-Books

E-books have some **drawbacks**, or problems. You need to buy a digital reader. You must also remember to charge the battery. This can be a big problem. If you forget to charge it, you cannot read the book.

The Winner Is...

It is not hard to figure out the best choice. With all of the benefits that e-books have, they are the clear winner!

GO ON →

Name: _____ Date: _____

Use "A Better Way to Read" to answer Numbers 1 through 5.

1 **Circle** the words that tell what an *analysis* is.

2 **Underline** two reasons the author gives for using e-books.

Write the name of the section that includes this information.

_____

3 **Circle** the word that gives the definition of *drawbacks*.

4 How does the author feel about charging the batteries of digital readers?

_____

_____

Underline a fact that supports this point of view.

5 What is the author's point of view about e-books?

_____

_____

Draw a box around the sentence that supports your answer.

STOP

Read "A King or a President?" before you answer Numbers 1 through 5.

A King or a President?

In 1776, American colonists announced their independence from Great Britain. They felt that King George had treated them unfairly. They were able to gain their freedom from England, but their new country was struggling. It needed a government and a leader.

The Great Debate

As a result, a **convention** was held in 1787. Its purpose was to make plans for a new government. Men from each state came to this meeting. They came to **debate**, or talk about, their ideas. They had a lot to discuss. How would the new leader be chosen? How much power would he have?

A Model Leader

Everyone agreed that the country needed a strong leader. Some people wanted a king. Others thought a king might have too much power. He could not be fired, and no one would have a say in choosing future kings. So they decided they wanted a new kind of leader. They wanted a president.

Therefore, the men decided to write a document—the Constitution. This document explains what the President of the United States can do and cannot do. The U.S. President's main job is to carry out the country's laws. Years ago, colonists believed a president could do a better job than a king. They were right!

GO ON →

Name: _____ **Date:** _____

Use "A King or a President?" to answer Numbers 1 through 5.

1 What problems did the country have after gaining its freedom?

_____

_____

Draw a box around the section that tells how people tried to solve these problems.

2 **Circle** the clues in the text that tell the meaning of *convention*.

What does *convention* mean?

_____

3 **Underline** the details that describe the problems some people saw with having a king.

4 **Circle** examples of questions the men came to *debate*.

What does *debate* mean?

_____

5 How did the Constitution solve some of the country's problems?

_____

_____

STOP

Read "The King's Favorite" before you answer Numbers 1 through 5.

The King's Favorite

Once, there was a village with two excellent bakers. One was jolly. He gave the village children treats, especially Polly.

The other baker was an unkind man. He always shooed the children out of his shop and never gave away his treats.

One day, the king's messenger came to the village. "Bakers, bring your best cake to the king," he announced. "He will taste them and **reveal** the name of the new royal baker."

The village children cheered for the jolly baker, but he was **unsure**. He did not know what to bake. "I do not know the king's favorite cake," he said.

The unkind baker gathered his ingredients. "My chocolate cake will win," he said. "It is the best in the land!"

Polly came running into the jolly baker's shop shouting, "I know the king's favorite." Then she whispered, "Lemon!"

The day of the contest arrived, and the king tasted the chocolate cake first. "Delicious!" he said as the unkind baker puffed out his chest with pride.

Next, the king tasted the jolly baker's cake. "Lemon! My favorite!" cried the king. "You," he pointed to the jolly baker, "are the new royal baker!"

The baker smiled at Polly. "Lemon!" he whispered.

GO ON →

Name: _____ Date: _____

Use "The King's Favorite" to answer Numbers 1 through 5.

1 **Underline** details that tell how the two bakers are alike.

How are they different?

_____

_____

2 **Circle** the details that tell what the king plans to *reveal*.

What does *reveal* mean?

_____

3 **Draw a box** around the details that show the unkind baker thinks he will win the contest.

How does the jolly baker feel about the contest?

_____

_____

4 **Circle** the details that show what *unsure* means.

5 How do the bakers act differently after the king tastes the cakes?

_____

_____

STOP

Read "Luther Burbank" before you answer Numbers 1 through 5.

Luther Burbank

Luther Burbank was born in 1849. His family had a farm. Burbank got his own farm when he was 22 years old. Farming was common back then, but Burbank was not a common farmer.

Burbank loved plants. He created a new type of potato in 1871 that is still the most used potato today. He sold the rights for $150. Then he moved to California. He spent his life there working with plants.

Burbank used new ways to grow plants. He attached parts from two different types of trees. They would grow together. The new tree had traits of both trees.

Burbank never called himself a scientist. He was an **energetic** and active gardener who loved plants. He was also creative. Burbank created more than 800 new plant types in his lifetime. These included flowers, fruits, vegetables, and grasses. His work **transformed** many plants so that they were different. He even grew a cactus that had no spines, or needles.

Burbank once said, "I love flowers, trees, animals, and all the works of nature as they pass before us in time and space." He died in 1926. Burbank is part of the National Inventors Hall of Fame.

GO ON →

Name: _____ Date: _____

Use "Luther Burbank" to answer Numbers 1 through 5.

1 **Draw a box** around the year that Burbank was born.

How many years later did he get his own farm?

_____

_____

2 **Underline** the sentence that tells when Burbank created a new type of potato.

Tell what Burbank did right after that.

_____

_____

3 **Circle** a clue in the text that helps you understand the meaning of *energetic*.

4 **Circle** details that tell how Burbank *transformed* a cactus plant.

What does *transformed* mean?

_____

_____

5 What did Burbank do when he was in California?

_____

_____

Underline the year he died.

STOP

Read "Anansi and the Snake" before you answer Numbers 1 through 5.

Anansi and the Snake

Once, there was a spider named Anansi. The animals of the forest made fun of him because he was so small. Anansi wanted them to respect him. He wanted them to look at him with **gratitude** and thanks.

So Anansi went home and made a plan. He decided that he would capture Snake, one of the longest, strongest animals in the forest.

The next day, Anansi went in **pursuit** of Snake with the hope of catching him. "Snake," called Anansi, "the other animals say you think you are the longest creature, but the shortest stick of bamboo is longer than you."

Snake came out of his house angrily. "I'll prove to them that I am the longest creature in the forest! Measure me!"

Anansi got out his ruler. "Wait," said Anansi. "If I start at your tail, how do I know you will not slide forward by the time I reach your head?"

"Tie my tail to that tree," said Snake. Once he was tied, Snake could not move, and so Anansi tied Snake's head to another tree. He had captured Snake!

"How clever you are!" the animals said. "We are sorry we made fun of you." From that day on, the animals treated Anansi with respect.

GO ON →

Name: _____ Date: _____

Use "Anansi and the Snake" to answer Numbers 1 through 5.

1 Why does Anansi make a plan?

_____

_____

2 **Circle** another word for *gratitude* in the passage.

3 **Draw a box** around the sentence that tells Anansi's plan.

What does this plan suggest about Anansi?

_____

4 **Circle** the clues that help you understand what *pursuit* means.

What is the meaning of *pursuit*?

_____

5 **Underline** the sentence that shows how the animals feel about Anansi at the end of the passage.

What is the message in the passage?

_____

_____

STOP

Read "Make a Difference!" before you answer Numbers 1 through 5.

Make a Difference!

A desk can make a difference—

To kids in Africa.

They sit on floors, and our desks—

Sit in America.

"Let's help!" I say to classmates.

"Let's make a plan today.

We'll plan to have a car wash.

And hold it Saturday!"

We earn some cash to send desks—

To kids in Africa.

We feel such satisfaction—

Here in America.

We're glad we made a difference.

We've helped our friends today.

Ambitious plans are needed.

Let's help another way!

Name: _____ **Date:** _____

Use "Make a Difference!" to answer Numbers 1 through 5.

1 **Underline** the dialogue in the first stanza.

How does this help you know the poem is narrative?

_____

_____

2 Write two words that rhyme from the end of the first stanza.

_____

3 **Circle** words that are repeated in the first and second stanza.

What does the speaker want you to think about by repeating these words?

_____

_____

4 **Draw a box** around details in the first and second stanza that tell what the speaker does to help.

5 How does the speaker make a difference in the world?

_____

_____

STOP

Name: _____ Date: _____

Read "A New Look" before you answer Numbers 1 through 5.

A New Look

"Grandpa will pick you up after school," said Mom.

Cara frowned; she loved her grandfather dearly, but she hoped he would not wear his usual outfit. He wore shorts and knee socks, even in winter. He also wore a funny hat with a feather. Cara never understood why he wore those odd clothes.

When Cara left class with her friend Yoshi, Grandpa was right outside. She looked away, embarrassed, as he said hello to Yoshi.

The next day, Yoshi said, "Your grandfather is great. I love the way he dresses."

Without thinking, Cara **blurted** out, "I wish he wouldn't wear those silly clothes in public!"

Yoshi said, "Your grandfather's clothes help to make him different and special. My grandmother used to live in Japan. She often wears beautiful, traditional dresses called *kimonos*. I really like that my grandmother is different from everyone else."

Cara thought about what her friend said. She no longer felt embarrassment. She had a new **appreciation** for her grandfather. Cara was now thankful and proud of his sense of style.

GO ON →

Use "A New Look" to answer Numbers 1 through 5.

1 How does Cara feel when she learns that her grandfather is picking her up after school?

_____

Underline the clues that show why she feels this way.

2 **Circle** the words that help you understand what *blurted* means.

What is the meaning of *blurted*?

_____

3 **Draw a box** around the details that show how Yoshi feels about her own background.

4 **Circle** the word that means the OPPOSITE of *appreciation*.

Which words in the text describe what *appreciation* means?

_____

5 What important lesson does Cara learn from Yoshi?

_____

_____

STOP

Read "Visiting Ancient Egypt" before you answer Numbers 1 through 5.

Visiting Ancient Egypt

Adam and his dad entered the museum and read the sign for the mummy exhibit. They both thought it was the best display in the museum.

"Let's go see the mummies!" said Adam. He loved to learn about ancient Egypt.

Suddenly, a strong wind swept past them and swirled in front of the exhibit's entrance. When it cleared, a wide river lay in its place. Adam and Dad were in an ancient **civilization**! There were no signs of a modern way of life.

It was getting dark fast. "We should build a shelter," said Dad. "Help me gather grasses and reeds along the river."

Adam had learned in school that ancient Egyptians used these plants to build things.

They had just **fashioned** a hut made from mud and reeds when a boy appeared.

"You have used our resources well," the boy said. "I will share a secret. At sunrise, follow the river north. You will find a man who will lead you back to your own time."

"Thank you, kind friend!" said Dad, but Adam was sad to end his adventure. It had been fun to use what he knew about nature.

GO ON →

Name: _____ Date: _____

Use "Visiting Ancient Egypt" to answer Numbers 1 through 5.

1 **Circle** the clues that show the meaning of *civilization*.

What does *civilization* mean?

_____

2 **Underline** the details that tell about the natural resources in the passage.

Why are these resources important to Adam and his dad?

_____

_____

3 **Circle** the details that describe what Adam and his dad *fashioned* together.

What does *fashioned* mean?

_____

4 **Draw a box** around the details that tell why the boy helps Adam and his dad at the end of the passage.

5 How do Adam's actions support the theme that learning about nature can be useful?

_____

_____

Read "Fibonacci Numbers" before you answer Numbers 1 through 5.

Fibonacci Numbers

Have you looked closely at objects in nature? Maybe you have noticed interesting patterns. Leonardo Fibonacci discovered a pattern again and again in nature. He saw this **repetition** in many objects, such as pinecones and seashells.

How the Pattern Works

The pattern is **visible** if you look at a sunflower. The seeds grow in a spiral shape. The center has one seed. The next part has two seeds. Add these numbers together, 1 + 2, to get 3. That is how many seeds you will find in the next part. Add the last two numbers each time to find the next number in the pattern.

How Plants Use the Pattern

Plants do not know about Fibonacci numbers, yet the pattern is there in the way leaves grow. You can even see it in the scales of a pineapple. Try to spot Fibonacci numbers the next time you are outside. You will be surprised to find it everywhere!

Fibonacci Number Spiral

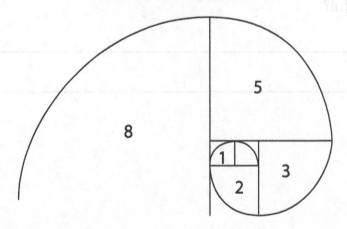

GO ON →

Name: _____ Date: _____

Use "Fibonacci Numbers" to answer Numbers 1 through 5.

1 **Circle** the clues that tell the meaning of *repetition*.

What does *repetition* mean?

_____

2 **Draw a box** around the key detail that tells where Fibonacci found patterns in nature.

3 **Circle** the clue in "How the Pattern Works" that tells where the Fibonacci pattern is *visible*.

What does *visible* mean?

_____

4 **Underline** the key detail that explains how to figure out the numbers in the Fibonacci number pattern.

Now use the Fibonacci number pattern to find the number that follows 8 in the diagram.

_____

5 What is the main idea of this article?

_____

_____

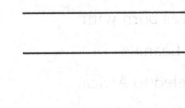

Read "Nick Kristof's Team" before you answer Numbers 1 through 5.

Nick Kristof's Team

Around the world, many people do not have medicines they need. In some places, women have few rights. Often, people work long hours in difficult conditions, making very little money. Nick Kristof is a journalist who writes about some of these problems. He hopes his writing will make others notice.

The Win-a-Trip Contest

Each year, Nick has a contest. He chooses one college student to travel with him. Like Nick, his hardworking partners have **dedicated** their time and effort to making the world a better place.

The partners study problems up close with Nick. They **collaborate**, working together closely to understand the problems. They interview people, take pictures, and write articles as ways of sharing their discoveries. Some groups donate money when they learn about these problems.

Nick's Student Partners

Leana Wen was one of Nick's partners. She was born with a serious form of asthma, which is a lung problem. Leana's illness made her want to become a doctor. She traveled to Africa with Nick. They made a movie about poverty and disease there.

Nick and his partners help us learn about problems that people face around the world. That's the first step in fixing them.

GO ON →

Name: _____ Date: _____

Use "Nick Kristof's Team" to answer Numbers 1 through 5.

1 **Underline** key details that tell about the problems Nick writes about.

2 **Circle** details that tell what Nick's partners have *dedicated* to making the world a better place.

What does *dedicated* mean?

_____

3 **Circle** clues that show how Nick's partners *collaborate* with him.

What does *collaborate* mean?

_____

4 **Draw a box** around key details that tell how Nick and his partners share their discoveries.

What happens when they share their discoveries?

_____

_____

5 **Underline** the details that tell how Leana Wen helped Nick.

What is the main idea of the section "Nick's Student Partners"?

_____

_____

STOP

Read "Mysteries of the Moai" before you answer Numbers 1 through 5.

Mysteries of the Moai

Easter Island in the Pacific Ocean is famous for incredible *moai* (moh•AY) statues, carved hundreds of years ago.

During that **era**, people did not have animals or wheels, so we do not know how the statues were moved. Some people believe the moai were dragged on tree trunks. Others think they were rolled on logs. The island people say, "The statues walked."

Scientists know there were not enough big trees to roll the statues. Statue **fragments** had also been found on the road. These pieces showed that the gigantic figures were standing upright when they were moved.

So, two scientists tested a theory: they rocked a statue side to side with ropes, and it slowly moved forward. This method needed just 18 people, which is not many at all. It showed that the island people were correct; the statues could "walk"!

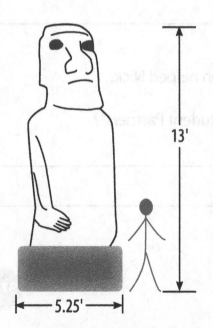

13'

5.25'

Measuring the Moai

Average height: 13 feet

Average width at base: 5.25 feet

Average weight: 14 tons

GO ON →

Name: _____ Date: _____

Use "Mysteries of the Moai" to answer Numbers 1 through 5.

1 How does the author feel about the moai?

_____

_____

Draw a box around the word that helps you know the author's point of view.

2 **Underline** the clues that tell about the *era* the statues were made.

What does *era* mean?

_____

_____

3 How do the details in the diagram support the author's point of view that the moai are "gigantic figures"?

_____

_____

4 **Underline** the clues that tell the meaning of *fragments*.

5 **Circle** the details that support the author's position that the moai could be moved using a "rocking" method.

STOP

Read "Calamity Jane" before you answer Numbers 1 through 5.

Calamity Jane

When Calamity Jane was born in Missouri, she looked just like a regular girl. Her name was Martha Jane Cannary. But she sure was special, for little Martha could ride a horse before she could even talk!

By the time she was in her teens, Martha was more than six feet tall! She bravely tamed wild broncos and hunted better than any man on this side of the Mississippi. When she was twenty, Martha joined the army. That's when her real adventures began.

To fit in, Martha dressed like a man. She wore a buckskin suit and leggings. Soon, she was given the nickname "Calamity Jane" because of her risky missions and daring **deeds**. There was no act too dangerous for this gal!

One act of courage happened while she was guarding a stagecoach in the Wild West. Suddenly, a band of outlaws came. They pushed the stagecoach into the river. With one toss of her lasso, Calamity Jane tied up all the outlaws so they could not escape. Then she jumped into the river and rescued every last person from the stagecoach!

Calamity Jane saved many lives. She also did plenty of **heroic** things. Her acts of bravery were known throughout the world. Stories are told about her to this very day!

GO ON →

Name: _____ Date: _____

Use "Calamity Jane" to answer Numbers 1 through 5.

1 **Underline** the clues in the first paragraph that show this passage is told from the third-person point of view.

2 **Draw a box** around the details in the first and second paragraphs that describe Calamity Jane.

What is one detail that is exaggerated and probably not true?

_____

_____

3 **Circle** the clues that tell the meaning of the word *deeds*.

What does *deeds* mean?

_____

4 What does the narrator think about Calamity Jane?

_____

_____

Underline the details in the fourth paragraph that support your answer.

5 **Circle** the words that help you understand the meaning of *heroic*.

What does *heroic* mean?

_____

STOP

Read "The Surprise" before you answer Numbers 1 through 5.

The Surprise

CAST

JADA and JON: sister and brother

GROUP: family and friends of Jada and Jon

Setting: A messy bedroom. JADA looks through her dresser drawers for her soccer photos and medals.

JADA: (*Looking **perplexed** and upset*) I don't understand. I can't find my soccer collection anywhere. I've been saving those photos and medals for years. Where are they?!

(*The next day, JADA leaves for soccer practice. She looks in JON'S room and sees a scrapbook, glue, and one of her photos.*)

JADA: (*Looking doubtful and mumbling to herself*) Now I'm getting **suspicious**. Jon is definitely up to something!

(*JADA comes home from soccer practice. She opens the front door of the house and turns on the light.*)

GROUP: (*Shouting*) Surprise! Happy Birthday!

(*JON walks up to JADA and hands her a gift-wrapped box.*)

JON: (*Smiling*) Here is my gift. I really hope you like it!

(*JADA unwraps the box and opens up the scrapbook.*)

JADA: (*Relieved and excited*) My soccer collection! Wow, everything looks even better in the scrapbook. Thank you so much, Jon. This is the best birthday present ever!

GO ON →

Name: _____ Date: _____

Use "The Surprise" to answer Numbers 1 through 5.

1 Who is the main speaker in the play?

_____

2 **Circle** the details that tell why Jada is *perplexed*.

What does *perplexed* mean?

_____

3 **Draw a box** around the stage direction that shows how Jada feels when she looks in Jon's room.

Which word tells how she feels?

_____

4 **Circle** the clues that show why Jada becomes *suspicious*.

What does *suspicious* mean?

_____

5 How does Jada feel at the end of the play?

_____

Underline the details that support your answer.

STOP

Read "Carrying on the Dream" before you answer Numbers 1 through 5.

Carrying on the Dream

Even as a young girl, Coretta Scott King was aware of **unequal** laws that were not fair. She had to walk five miles to go to a one-room school. White children rode school buses to go to a school that was much closer.

While she was in college, Coretta joined a civil rights group. She met Martin Luther King, Jr. That is when her life changed. In 1953, they were married. Coretta worked with her husband to peacefully fight for equal rights. Together, they helped to get the Civil Rights Act passed in 1964.

When Dr. King was killed in 1968, Coretta carried on her husband's dream. In 1969, she wrote a book called *My Life With Martin Luther King, Jr.* Coretta continued to be **outspoken** about important causes. She spoke openly about social issues and wrote a newspaper column.

Coretta spent years planning a memorial for her husband. In 1980, a historic site was created in Atlanta, Georgia. Coretta served as the president of the new King Center. It has a library with a large collection of civil rights documents.

Coretta also fought to get a national holiday in her husband's name. Today, more than 100 countries celebrate Dr. King's birthday. Sadly, Coretta passed away in 2006. Her work still inspires many people today.

GO ON →

Name: _____ Date: _____

Use "Carrying on the Dream" to answer Numbers 1 through 5.

1 Which clues in the text tell the meaning of *unequal*?

_____

2 **Draw a box** around the text that tells Coretta's views about equal rights.

How does the author probably feel about equal rights?

_____

_____

_____

3 What is the author's point of view about Martin Luther King, Jr.?

_____

_____

_____

4 **Circle** the words that tell how Coretta was *outspoken*.

What does *outspoken* mean?

_____

_____

5 **Underline** the details in the last paragraph that describe Coretta Scott King.

What does the author think about her?

_____

_____

_____

STOP

Name: _____ **Date:** _____

Read "From Windmills to Wind Farms" before you answer Numbers 1 through 5.

From Windmills to Wind Farms

For centuries, people have depended on wind energy to meet their needs. Windmills pumped water in ancient China. Farmers used windmills to grind wheat and corn. Modern windmills create electricity for homes and businesses.

Energy Use

In the 1970s, there was not a lot of oil available in the U.S. People counted on oil as a source of energy, so finding a replacement became a **necessity**. The U.S. government looked for different energy sources. Today, scientists must continue to look for new resources. They want to **conserve** natural resources because we must protect what is left of coal and oil. Otherwise, they may soon disappear. Wind is a good energy source to have because we will never run out of it.

Farming the Wind

Many wind farms are being built across the country. The farms have machines called *turbines*. Wind spins the turbine blades to create energy and make electricity.

Wind farms are now being built in oceans because of the strong breezes there. Oceans are a good place to produce this type of energy. There are no buildings or trees to block the wind.

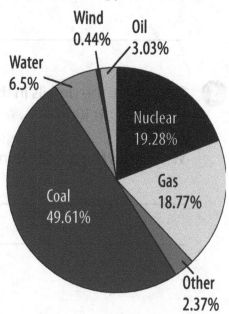

Use of Energy in the U.S.

Wind 0.44%
Oil 3.03%
Water 6.5%
Nuclear 19.28%
Coal 49.61%
Gas 18.77%
Other 2.37%

GO ON →

Weekly Assessment · Unit 4, Week 4

Name: _____ Date: _____

Use "From Windmills to Wind Farms" to answer Numbers 1 through 5.

1 What is the author's point of view about wind energy?

_____

_____

Underline the details that support your answer.

2 **Circle** the details that tell why finding new energy sources became a *necessity* in the 1970s.

What does *necessity* mean?

_____

3 **Draw a box** around the details supporting the author's point of view that ocean wind farms are a good idea.

4 **Circle** the word that has almost the same meaning as *conserve*.

5 How does the chart support the author's point of view that scientists must continue to look for new resources?

_____

_____

STOP

Read "My Skateboard and Me" before you answer Numbers 1 through 5.

My Skateboard and Me

Helmet, safety gear—all on and secured.

Perched high upon the ramp, I look down.

I breathe in. . . I breathe out. . . I take off!

Soaring like a bird through the air—wind whipping hair.

I am joined to my skateboard; my board is part of me.

We are one . . . halves of each other . . . the same.

I am soulful and serious, both daredevil and dreamer.

Skating is an expression, a way for me to communicate.

Falling. . . flying. . . free!

Every move I make—meaningful and important.

Twisting and turning, stretching and straining.

I breathe in. . . I breathe out. . . I make this sweet ride last.

GO ON →

Use "My Skateboard and Me" to answer Numbers 1 through 5.

1 Explain how you know this is a free verse poem.

_____

_____

2 **Draw a box** around the details that tell how the speaker and the skateboard are the same.

3 **Underline** the details in the third stanza that tell how the speaker feels while skateboarding.

What are the speaker's feelings toward skateboarding?

_____

_____

4 **Circle** the examples of alliteration in the last stanza of the poem.

Tell what the speaker describes in this stanza.

_____

_____

5 What is the poem's main message?

_____

_____

_____

STOP

Read "Practicing Friendship" before you answer Numbers 1 through 5.

Practicing Friendship

As Sanjay walked toward the school bus, Tom said, "I wish I could play hockey like you do. Do you think you could show me how to pass and shoot on the ice today?"

Sanjay was quiet, for he knew that if he helped Tom, he would not be able to stay **focused** on his own practice. Paying attention to hockey was important to Sanjay. The kids at school thought he was a **superb** skater, better than anyone they had ever seen. But Sanjay knew that the kids at the hockey rink were all good, and he had to work extra hard to impress them. "Sorry, I'm pretty busy," he replied.

"It's okay, I understand," said Tom, although he wasn't sure he did.

An hour later, Sanjay had finished practicing and was thinking about Tom's question earlier. He shouted across the rink, "Hey, Tom, I can help you with some goal shots now."

But it was too late, and Tom shrugged and mumbled, "Thanks, but George and I have been working together on it. He was a great help, and I even made a goal!" he added.

Sanjay asked hopefully, "Maybe another time?"

Tom shrugged and said, "Maybe."

"I may be a great skater," thought Sanjay, "but I have something new to practice—being a much better friend."

GO ON →

Name: _____ Date: _____

Use "Practicing Friendship" to answer Numbers 1 through 5.

1 **Underline** the details that show how Tom feels about Sanjay when they first walk out of school.

2 **Circle** the clues that tell what Sanjay must do to stay *focused*.

What does *focused* mean?

_____

3 **Draw a box** around the details that show how Tom feels about Sanjay at the ice rink.

How have Tom's feelings changed?

_____

_____

4 **Circle** the details that show why the kids at school think Sanjay is a *superb* skater.

What does *superb* mean?

_____

5 **Underline** the details that tell what Sanjay thinks to himself on the ice rink at the end of the passage.

Explain how Sanjay will probably act differently in the future.

_____

_____

STOP

Read "The Lowell Girls Strike" before you answer Numbers 1 through 5.

The Lowell Girls Strike

Emily's shoulders ached as she stood at the cloth loom, but she did not stop working. She did not want to seem like a **weakling** on her first day at the Lowell Mill. At 10, Emily was the youngest worker, but she expected no **sympathy**. The other girls would not take pity on her as they, too, worked hard.

That evening in the factory housing, several girls whispered, "It's not right—no person should have to work 14 hours a day! We should strike."

"I don't know," Clara remarked with a frown. "Remember when we complained about paying extra for our meals? Nothing happened then, so what makes you think it will now?"

"I still say we strike," announced Sarah as the other girls chimed in, "Strike, Strike!"

On Thursday, the workers refused to start their machines. When the factory boss arrived, Sarah handed him a letter with thousands of signatures demanding a shorter workday.

For two weeks, the girls refused to work, and they wondered nervously if they would lose their jobs. Finally, Sarah cried, "Our workday has been reduced to 11 hours!"

Everyone cheered, and Clara said, "It's a fine start."

Emily smiled and followed the crowd back to work. Already, her shoulders felt better.

GO ON →

Name: _____ Date: _____

Use "The Lowell Girls Strike" to answer Numbers 1 through 5.

1 What do Emily and the other girls have in common?

_____

_____

2 **Underline** the clues that help you understand the meaning of *weakling*.

What does *weakling* mean?

_____

3 **Underline** the sentence that tells why Emily does not expect *sympathy*.

What is the meaning of *sympathy*?

_____

4 How is Clara different from the other girls in the group?

_____

_____

5 **Draw a box** around the details that show how Emily feels at the end of the passage.

How do her feelings change in the passage?

_____

_____

STOP

Name: _____ Date: _____

Read "Keeping the Oceans Quiet" before you answer Numbers 1 through 5.

Keeping the Oceans Quiet

Scientists have worried about saving whales for years, but now they have a new concern—protecting the animals' hearing!

Long ago, most ocean noises came from waves and weather; in contrast, today the ocean is **noticeably** louder than in the past. Large machines and other manmade sources create much more noise pollution.

A whale's hearing is its most important sense. Whales use sound to communicate, and they depend on their hearing to locate food and their families. Loud noises **impact** their hearing and affect their ability to use it.

Scientists want to reduce noise pollution. They are making maps that show what and where the loud noises are. In the near future, they hope to limit noise levels allowed in oceans.

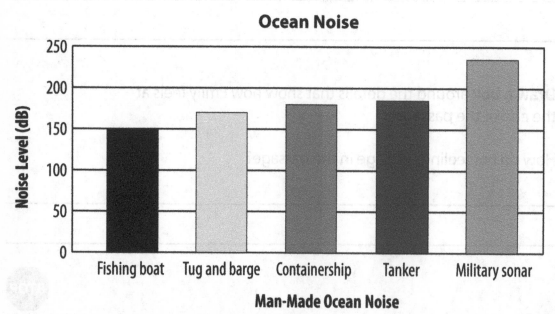

Ocean Noise

Noise Level (dB) / Man-Made Ocean Noise: Fishing boat, Tug and barge, Containership, Tanker, Military sonar

GO ON →

Name: _____ Date: _____

Use "Keeping the Oceans Quiet" to answer Numbers 1 through 5.

1 **Circle** details that describe what scientists have been concerned about for years.

What are they concerned about now?

_____

2 **Underline** the words that help to show what *noticeably* means.

Write the meaning of *noticeably*.

_____

3 How are ocean noises today different from in the past?

_____

_____

4 **Underline** the sentence that tells how ocean noises *impact* whales.

What does *impact* mean?

_____

5 Look at the bar graph. **Draw a box** around the name of the machine that creates the most ocean noise.

STOP

Read "Isaac Newton's Science" before you answer Numbers 1 through 5.

Isaac Newton's Science

Legend says that one day an apple dropped on Sir Isaac Newton's head as he sat under a tree. This made Newton notice gravity, the force that pulls objects toward Earth.

No one knows for sure if the apple story is true. However, something made Newton pay attention to forces in nature. Today the science of physics is based on his ideas.

Newton and the Universe

Newton was a student during the 1660s. When the university closed for several years, he took time to explore his own ideas about math and physics. As a result, Newton learned about how the universe works. He studied **astronomical** theories, including the movement of objects in outer space. He examined what makes the Moon **orbit**, or go around, Earth.

Newton's Laws

You may be familiar with Newton's Laws. One is that objects at rest stay at rest unless acted upon by a force. Another is that every action has an opposite and equal reaction.

Much of our knowledge about the universe today is thanks to Newton.

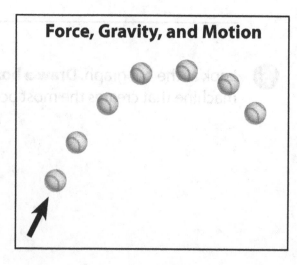

Force, Gravity, and Motion

GO ON →

Name: _____ Date: _____

Use "Isaac Newton's Science" to answer Numbers 1 through 5.

1 **Underline** the details that tell what caused Newton to first notice gravity.

2 **Draw a box** around the event that caused Newton to explore his own ideas.

What did he learn as a result of his studies?

_____

_____

3 **Circle** the words that tell what *astronomical* theories are.

What does *astronomical* mean?

_____

_____

4 Which words in the article tell the meaning of *orbit*?

_____

_____

5 Look at the diagram. According to Newton's theories, what will the force of gravity cause the ball to do?

_____

_____

Name: _____ Date: _____

Read "The Problem of E-Waste" before you answer Numbers 1 through 5.

The Problem of E-Waste

E-waste, or electronic waste, is made up of electronics that get thrown away. The problem of e-waste has grown quickly through the years, and it does not have an easy solution.

Problems with Dumping E-Waste

Each U.S. family owns about 25 different electronics. We only recycle about 14% of these, so most are thrown away in landfills. This creates a **widespread** problem around the world. As electronics sit in landfills, their chemicals poison the ground.

The Case Against Recycling

Recycling e-waste has problems, too, because too much from the U.S. is sent to other countries. As workers take apart these machines, unsafe chemicals are released into the air. The chemicals reach **agricultural** areas and poison the soil and crops.

What Is the Solution?

More laws are needed to make sure electronics are recycled safely. People should also think carefully before buying the next new product. After all, the less we buy, the less waste we create!

The Facts About E-Waste	
E-Waste Issue	**Data**
• Average lifespan for electronics	• 2 to 4 years
• Amount of e-scrap recycled in the U.S. in 2010	• 300 million pounds
• E-waste created each year around the world	• 20 to 50 million tons
• Expected amount of e-waste in 15 years	• 7 times current amount

GO ON →

Name: _____ Date: _____

Use "The Problem of E-Waste" to answer Numbers 1 through 5.

1 **Underline** the facts in the article that tell about the amount of electronics in the U.S.

How do these facts support the author's point of view that e-waste is a problem?

_____

_____

2 **Circle** the words that show e-waste is a *widespread* problem.

What does *widespread* mean?

_____

3 **Draw a box** around the evidence that explains why recycling e-waste is also a problem.

4 **Circle** the words that describe *agricultural* areas.

What does *agricultural* mean?

_____

5 How does the chart support the author's points about e-waste?

_____

_____

Underline the solutions that the author suggests at the end of the article.

STOP

Read "For My Country" before you answer Numbers 1 through 5.

For My Country

I'll never forget President Kennedy's words: *ask not what your country can do for you—ask what you can do for your country.*

I took those words to heart. Now, I am here in Africa with my old classmate, Gary. We signed up to volunteer in another country.

After getting our college degrees, we joined the Peace Corps in 1963. The Peace Corps is a service organization that the President began. We wanted to make **contributions**, and now we help to educate children in Ghana.

As new **recruits**, we spent the first three months learning about African culture, how to manage a classroom, and getting kids excited about learning. This is our second year teaching.

"Where shall we take the kids next week?" I asked Gary.

"How about the nearby national park?" he suggested. "Taking them out of the classroom is the best way to learn about nature."

I agreed, and the kids love exploring Ghana's rainforests.

When we aren't teaching, Gary and I are helping local families plant crops. I now understand the Peace Corps' motto and why this work is "the toughest job you'll ever love." My work is difficult, but completely worth it. I will always remember my time here and the people I helped along the way.

GO ON →

Name: _____ Date: _____

Use "For My Country" to answer Numbers 1 through 5.

1 **Draw a box** around the details that show how the narrator feels about President Kennedy's words.

Explain what these words mean to the narrator.

_____

_____

2 **Circle** the clues that describe the narrator's *contributions*.

What is the meaning of *contributions*?

_____

3 Explain why the narrator and his friend go to Ghana.

_____

_____

4 **Circle** the details that tell what the narrator and his friend do as new *recruits*.

What does *recruits* mean?

_____

5 **Underline** the details that show the meaning of the Peace Corps' motto: the toughest job you'll ever love.

_____

STOP

Read "Lost and Found" before you answer Numbers 1 through 5.

Lost and Found

Randy rode his bike into the schoolyard just as a group of kids on the basketball team were leaving the court. As he took off his **protective** helmet and locked up his bike, he noticed a basketball on the ground. When he picked it up and spun it around, he saw that it was signed by a professional player.

"This ball is valuable!" he thought. Randy was not on the basketball team, but he loved playing ball. Unfortunately, he just didn't have time in his schedule to play.

Randy thought about keeping the basketball—but only for a moment, for he knew it was his responsibility to find the owner. Throughout the day, he asked other students who might own it. Their responses made Randy feel **confident** that the ball belonged to Derrick, the captain of the basketball team. Now that he was sure, Randy approached Derrick after school.

"I think this belongs to you," said Randy.

"Thanks!" said Derrick, looking very relieved. "Where did you find it?"

"By the practice court," said Randy as he handed Derrick the ball. "I'm Randy, by the way."

Derrick smiled and asked, "How about shooting some hoops with me?"

Randy was happy to get some ball time, so the two new friends strolled toward the court together.

GO ON →

Name: _____ **Date:** _____

Use "Lost and Found" to answer Numbers 1 through 5.

1 **Underline** the word that helps you know what
protective means.

What is the meaning of *protective*?

_____

2 **Circle** what Randy thinks about doing at first when he finds
the basketball.

3 **Draw a box** around the text that tells why Randy tries to find
the owner of the basketball.

How does Derrick feel when he gets the ball back?

_____

_____

4 **Underline** the text evidence that tells why Randy feels *confident*
that the ball belongs to Derrick.

What does *confident* mean?

_____

5 Write a sentence that tells the main message of the passage.

_____

_____

STOP

Read "I've Got My Eye on You!" before you answer Numbers 1 through 5.

I've Got My Eye on You!

Animals go through physical changes to survive in their environment. One **adaptation** is improved eyesight, which is found in both predators and prey.

Amazing Night Vision

One predator with incredible eyesight is the owl. It has huge eyes that can see very well at night when it hunts for food. An owl's head can also turn around to face almost completely backward, allowing it to spot prey from almost any direction.

Another predator is the everyday housecat, which may look harmless, but is actually a skilled hunter. If you have a pet cat, then you know that it is often very active at night. That is because it, too, has highly developed night vision. The pupil in a cat's eye can expand to a large circle to allow more light inside. This almost doubles a cat's ability to see in the dark.

Perfect Placement

Predators may have amazing eyes, but animals of prey have also adapted well to survive. They do not have forward-facing eyes, like humans. Instead, their eyes face sideways, allowing them to view a wider area at once. This helps them avoid surprise attacks by predators while they **forage**, or look for food on the ground.

So, the next time you are outside, know that an animal might have its eye on you!

GO ON →

Name: _____ Date: _____

Use "I've Got My Eye on You!" to answer Numbers 1 through 5.

1 **Circle** the definition of an animal *adaptation*.

2 **Underline** the sentence that describes the way an owl sees.

Why can owls spot prey so easily?

_____

_____

3 **Draw a box** around the detail that tells why a cat is able to see so well in the dark.

What do you think is the effect of having this ability?

_____

_____

4 Why do animals of prey have eyes that face sideways?

_____

_____

5 **Circle** the clues that show what animals do when they *forage*.

What does *forage* mean?

_____

STOP

Read "Teddy Roosevelt, Environmental President" before you answer Numbers 1 through 5.

Teddy Roosevelt, Environmental President

In a 1907 address, President Theodore Roosevelt showed his concern for the environment:

We are prone to speak of the resources of this country as inexhaustible; this is not so.

What Roosevelt meant was that natural resources are limited and rules must be put in place before these resources run out. So, Roosevelt **urged** people in government to pass environment laws, asking them to save our lands.

Between 1901 and 1909, Roosevelt took action to protect almost 230 million acres of land! This amount of land is the size of all of the states on the East Coast, from Florida to Maine.

Roosevelt also signed the National Monuments Act. This legislation protects the beautiful **landscape** of the Grand Canyon. Some of Roosevelt's achievements also included the creation of five national parks, 18 national monuments, and 150 national forests. In addition, he solved the problem of what to do with land that had been destroyed. He started 21 projects that helped to renew land so it would become useful again.

Some of Roosevelt's greatest achievements were in helping our planet. Many people remember him as the country's environmental President.

GO ON →

Name: _____ Date: _____

Use "Teddy Roosevelt, Environmental President" to answer Numbers 1 through 5.

1 **Underline** the details that describe the environmental problem President Roosevelt identified.

2 **Circle** the clues that show how Roosevelt *urged* the government to solve the problem.

What does *urged* mean?

_____

_____

3 **Draw a box** around the details that show Roosevelt's solutions to the environmental problem.

4 **Circle** an example of a *landscape* Roosevelt protected.

What does *landscape* mean?

_____

_____

5 How are Roosevelt's beliefs still important today?

_____

_____

_____

Underline the text evidence that supports your answer.

STOP

Read "E-Pen Pals Forever!" before you answer Numbers 1 through 5.

E-Pen Pals Forever!

My best friend, Pang, moved back to China on a rainy day

last June. On that day, both the clouds and I shed a few tears.

"When will I see you again?

How will we keep a connection?"

Pang told me not to worry, that we could stay close

by being e-pen pals. "That's just not the same!" I wailed.

It's been six months now, and we e-mail each week.

We exchange photos; we share the special things we're doing.

She greets me by saying, "Ni Hao;" I say, "Hi there!"

I'm learning new expressions—my favorite is "Ni chi fan le ma?"

or "Have you eaten rice yet?" That's how people greet each other

because rice is eaten at every meal,

whether it's boiled, steamed, or fried.

It's just like eating bread here,

whether it's sliced, buttered, or rolled.

Now it's mid-January and the New Year has passed.

Pang is celebrating the Chinese New Year, dancing in parades

among thousands of smiling, shining lanterns. Pang's family

has invited me to visit next year during the Chinese New Year!

I can't wait! Being e-pen pals isn't so bad. We stay connected

halfway across the world—two friends, two cultures to share!

GO ON →

Use "E-Pen Pals Forever!" to answer Numbers 1 through 5.

1 **Underline** the words in the first stanza that help you know how the speaker feels.

2 **Draw a box** around the words in the second stanza that are an example of assonance.

3 How do you know that this is a narrative poem?

_____

_____

4 **Circle** the details that tell what the speaker likes learning from Pang.

5 Tell how the speaker feels at the end of the poem about being e-pen pals.

_____

_____

Underline the details in the text that support your answer.

STOP

Mid-Unit Assessment

Read "The Place to Be" before you answer Numbers 1 through 5.

The Place to Be

After school, Marco and Pete walked home. They took turns dribbling a basketball.

"I wish we had a place to shoot baskets," said Pete. "Land is **scarce** in the city. It is hard to find a place to play! If we had a basketball court in our neighborhood, we could play any time we wanted!"

The boys were passing by the grocery store when suddenly, Marco pointed to the distance.

"Look, an empty lot!" he said. "It's the perfect size for a basketball court! Let's ask Mrs. Flores who owns it."

"Hello, boys!" smiled Mrs. Flores. The storeowner was busy arranging a display.

"Do you know who owns that empty lot across the street?" asked Marco.

"Why, I do! I can't decide what to do with it. The lot is too small to build apartments."

Marco and Pete shared their idea with Mrs. Flores.

"That's a great idea!" she said. "I would enjoy having kids like you play there every day."

The next day, Mrs. Flores called city officials and donated the land for the project. Marco and Pete stopped by that afternoon, and she shared the good news with them.

Pete and Marco high-fived each other *and* Mrs. Flores.

GO ON →

"But what do we do now?" frowned Pete. "We don't have money to build the court!"

"Don't worry, boys!" she smiled. "Wait here while I make a phone call."

Mrs. Flores was smiling when she came back.

"My brother, Tony, owns a construction company. He will donate the materials and build the court if you boys are willing to help him."

The boys helped the crew every weekend. Their friends pitched in, too. Once the court was completed, the workers built park benches. After construction was done, there was still some empty land behind the court. Marco suggested that they build a mini-park. Then the younger kids could have a place to play, too.

On opening day, everybody in the neighborhood came. The younger kids played in the mini-park, the older kids played basketball, and the parents sat on the benches and watched. From that day on, Mrs. Flores's empty lot became *the* place to be!

GO ON →

Name: _____ **Date:** _____

Use "*The* Place to Be" to answer Numbers 1 through 5.

1 Read this sentence from the passage.

> "Land is scarce in the city."

Which sentence from the passage gives a clue about the meaning of *scarce*?

Ⓐ After school, Marco and Pete walked home.

Ⓑ "It is hard to find a place to play!"

Ⓒ "It's the perfect size for a basketball court! "

2 What problem do Marco and Pete have at the beginning of the passage?

Ⓐ They do not have time to play basketball.

Ⓑ They do not have a place to play basketball.

Ⓒ They do not have friends to play basketball with.

3 Who helps Marco and Pete solve their problem?

Ⓐ the boys' parents

Ⓑ a group of school friends

Ⓒ Mrs. Flores, the storeowner

GO ON →

4 What is needed after Mrs. Flores donates the land for the boys' project?

Ⓐ a space large enough for a basketball court

Ⓑ money and materials to build with

Ⓒ park benches for parents to sit on

5 Which event happens last in the passage?

Ⓐ The community enjoys the new basketball court and mini-park.

Ⓑ The workers build a basketball court, park benches, and a mini-court.

Ⓒ The boys discover an empty lot that would make a great basketball court.

GO ON →

Read "The Story of Surfing" before you answer Numbers 6 through 10.

The Story of Surfing

A Polynesian Start

The story of surfing began more than 3,000 years ago in Polynesia. This is a large group of islands in the southern Pacific Ocean. Long ago, the fishermen in Polynesia used wooden boards to ride giant waves. These fishermen had a purpose. They would surf toward the shore. There, they laid their catch of the day on the sand.

The explorer Captain James Cook arrived in 1769. He saw a man paddling quickly in a small canoe. The man then stopped. He sat very still. Suddenly, a giant wave swept up the canoe! The man surfed along at the same speed as the wave. He landed on the beach.

Cook thought it looked like a lot of fun. He thought the man must have felt the "most supreme pleasure" from surfing in this way.

Surfing in Hawaii

The Polynesians brought surfing to Hawaii, too. It became popular there. Even royalty loved it! During the 1800s, King Kamehameha I was the ruler of the Big Island. He used a hardwood surfboard. It was called *olo*. The board was about 24 feet long!

The king could **navigate** big waves. He skillfully steered his board with his legs and feet. He used his arms to balance. The king showed great skill. Today, surfing is often called the "Sport of Kings!"

GO ON →

The Father of Modern Surfing

In the early 1900s, there was a young man named Duke Kahanamoku who lived in Hawaii. He enjoyed surfing there on Waikiki Beach. He was also a talented swimmer. Duke won medals at three different Olympics! He is often considered the father of modern surfing.

Duke helped to make surfing popular in the United States. He once said:

Every day of the year where the water is 76 (degrees)...and the waves roll high, I take my sled...and coast down the face of the big waves that roll in at Waikiki.

The people of Hawaii still enjoy surfing today. Many **generations** of families carry on the tradition. Parents teach their children. Children teach *their* children. Surfing is an important part of culture in Hawaii. People of all ages enjoy riding the waves.

GO ON →

Name: _____ Date: _____

Use "The Story of Surfing" to answer Numbers 6 through 10.

6 Fishermen rode the waves in Polynesia thousands of years ago because it was _____.

Ⓐ a lot of fun to do

Ⓑ a way to bring fish to shore

Ⓒ a new sport they were learning

7 What happened when the man that Captain Cook was watching stopped paddling his canoe?

Ⓐ The canoe drifted further away from the beach.

Ⓑ The canoe started moving backwards in the water.

Ⓒ A wave swept up the canoe and carried it to shore.

8 Read this sentence from the article.

The king could navigate big waves.

Which evidence from the article helps to explain the meaning of *navigate*?

Ⓐ He skillfully steered his board with his legs and feet.

Ⓑ He used his arms to balance.

Ⓒ Today, surfing is often called "The Sport of Kings!"

GO ON →

9 According to the quote by Duke Kahanamoku, surfing reminds him of _____.

Ⓐ canoeing

Ⓑ sledding

Ⓒ swimming

10 Read this sentence from the article.

Many generations of families carry on the tradition.

Which sentence from the article gives a clue about the meaning of *generations*?

Ⓐ The people of Hawaii still enjoy surfing today.

Ⓑ Parents teach their children.

Ⓒ Surfing is an important part of culture in Hawaii.

STOP

Read "The Way to Her Heart" before you answer Numbers 1 through 4.

The Way to Her Heart

Once upon a time, there was a prince who walked to the market every day. On his return to the castle, he would pass through a meadow. Each time, he saw the same beautiful young woman picking flowers. One day, he approached her.

"My name is Princess Ana," said the woman when the prince asked her name.

The prince was delighted that she was royalty. "May I call on you tomorrow?"

"My father, the king, would not approve. He wants me to marry a prince who lives in a faraway land."

"But I am a prince, and I live in the next village! How can I convince him?"

"Find a gift worthy of my love and my father's respect," she suggested.

The next day, the prince set out to find the princess a gift. Soon, he met a goldsmith.

"I am looking for a gift worthy of a princess," he said. "It must impress her father, too."

"Here is a crate filled with gold for your **consideration**," said the goldsmith. "It will show your great wealth!"

The prince thought about it and made a decision. "This is not what I am looking for."

The prince continued on. Next, the prince shared his story with a jewelry maker.

GO ON →

"Here is a valuable necklace made of diamonds," said the jewelry maker. "It will capture the princess's heart."

Again, the prince declined, and he sadly returned home empty-handed.

As he traveled across the meadow, he had an idea. In a **flurry** of excitement, he rushed about and picked a bunch of flowers. Then, he tied them together with a velvet ribbon.

The prince went to the princess's castle and met the king and his daughter in the great hall. The prince bowed to the king.

"I have come to call on your daughter. I did not think a crate of gold or a diamond necklace were worthy of her."

He handed the princess the flowers.

"These flowers capture your daughter's beauty: the blue of her eyes, the red of her lips, the yellow of her hair."

The princess looked at the king and smiled. "This prince understands the way to my heart," she said.

Princess Ana took the prince's hand and they married with the king's blessing. They lived happily ever after.

GO ON →

Use "The Way to Her Heart" to answer Numbers 1 through 4.

1 Read this sentence from the passage.

> **"Here is a crate filled with gold for your consideration," said the goldsmith.**

Which sentence from the passage helps to explain what *consideration* means?

Ⓐ "It must impress her father, too."

Ⓑ The prince thought about it and made a decision.

Ⓒ "This is not what I am looking for."

2 Which problem does the prince find with the crate of gold and the necklace?

Ⓐ They are not worthy of the princess.

Ⓑ They are gifts the princess already owns.

Ⓒ They are not what the princess has asked for.

GO ON →

3 Read these sentences from the passage.

> As he traveled across the meadow, he had an idea.
> In a flurry of excitement, he rushed about and
> picked a bunch of flowers.

Which phrase from the sentences gives a clue about the meaning of *flurry*?

Ⓐ traveled across

Ⓑ had an idea

Ⓒ rushed about

4 At the end of the passage, what does the prince compare to the beauty of the princess?

Ⓐ diamonds

Ⓑ flowers

Ⓒ gold

GO ON →

Read "A President for Peace" before you answer Numbers 5 through 10.

A President for Peace

Jimmy Carter was 39th President of the United States. He has dedicated his life to solving problems. The former President still **consults** with world leaders today. He seeks out their advice and information to try to help solve world problems.

Early Life

James Earl Carter, Jr., was born on October 1, 1924. His father owned a farm in Georgia. Young Jimmy worked hard on the family farm.

Jimmy became interested in business early in life. He began selling his farm's peanuts. He used the money to buy five cotton bales. He was only 9 years old! He saved the cotton bales. Years later, the bales were worth a lot of money. Jimmy sold the cotton bales. He used this money to buy homes. He rented the homes to farm workers.

Jimmy completed high school. He was the first person in his family to do so. Then he joined the U.S. Navy. Carter became a Naval officer. During this time, he married Rosalynn Smith. Rosalynn was his sister's best friend.

Public Service

In the early 1960s, Carter became interested in politics. He began serving as Georgia state senator in 1963. In 1971, Carter became governor. During this time, African Americans did not have the same rights as whites. Carter supported equal rights for African Americans. He passed laws in favor of racial equality. He also made sure that more African Americans were in public office.

GO ON →

Promoting Peace

Governor Carter decided to run for U.S. President. In 1976, he campaigned against President Ford. It was a close race, but Carter won. He became President in 1977.

During his presidency, Carter worked to end conflicts between countries. In 1977, he met with world leaders from Israel and Egypt. He helped to create a peace plan between the two nations.

In 2002, Carter was awarded the Nobel Peace Prize. He received the honor for his dedication to peace, democracy, and human rights.

Steps Toward Peace

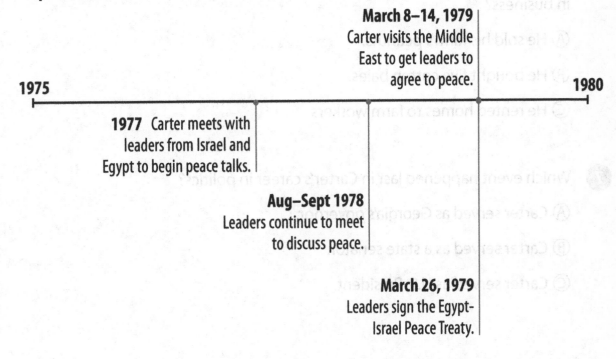

March 8–14, 1979
Carter visits the Middle East to get leaders to agree to peace.

1975   1980

1977 Carter meets with leaders from Israel and Egypt to begin peace talks.

Aug–Sept 1978
Leaders continue to meet to discuss peace.

March 26, 1979
Leaders sign the Egypt-Israel Peace Treaty.

GO ON →

Use "A President for Peace" to answer Numbers 5 through 10.

5 Read this sentence from the article.

> **The former President still consults with world leaders today.**

Which phrase from the article helps to explain the meaning of *consults*?

Ⓐ dedicated his life to solving problems

Ⓑ seeks out their advice and information

Ⓒ try to solve world problems

6 Which event tells how Carter first became interested in business?

Ⓐ He sold his farm's peanuts.

Ⓑ He bought five cotton bales.

Ⓒ He rented homes to farm workers

7 Which event happened last in Carter's career in politics?

Ⓐ Carter served as Georgia's governor.

Ⓑ Carter served as a state senator.

Ⓒ Carter served as U.S. President.

GO ON →

Name: _____ Date: _____

8 Which sentence is NOT an example of how Carter worked to solve the problem of racial inequality?

Ⓐ He passed laws in favor of racial equality.

Ⓑ He began serving as Georgia state senator in 1963.

Ⓒ He made sure that more African Americans were in public office.

9 Which evidence from the text tells how Carter solved a problem during his time as President?

Ⓐ He served as a Naval officer after completing the Naval Academy.

Ⓑ He rented homes that he owned to farm workers.

Ⓒ He met with world leaders to create peace plans.

10 According to the time line, when was a peace treaty signed between Egypt and Israel?

Ⓐ 1977

Ⓑ 1978

Ⓒ 1979

STOP

Read "One Wild Ride!" before you answer Numbers 1 through 5.

One Wild Ride!

The Alvarez family parked their car near an open field. Hugo carried a picnic basket, and his mother and sister carried backpacks filled with items they would need for their ride. Hugo's father was checking on the hot-air balloon. Mr. Alvarez just got his pilot's license, and he was taking his family on their first balloon ride!

The family piled into the large basket. Once they were safely inside, the balloon started rising up, up, and away!

"Wow! This is the coolest flying machine I've ever seen!" Hugo grinned.

Mom laughed. "I think I left my stomach on the ground!"

"Look!" Eva pointed. "I think we're headed toward that mountain."

Mr. Alvarez had just guided the balloon over the mountain when suddenly, a thick fog surrounded them.

"It's hard to see!" shouted Mr. Alvarez. "This could be a serious problem. It's **critical** that I try to land the balloon."

"I see land ahead!" shouted Hugo.

At that moment, the family heard a ripping sound, and the basket landed on the ground with a *plop*.

"Is everyone all right?" asked Mr. Alvarez.

The fog lifted and everyone looked around.

"Where are we?" asked Hugo. "All of the plants are huge! I think we landed on another planet!"

GO ON →

Mrs. Alvarez chimed in, "Let's get out of here quickly. If the plants are this big, I don't want to know what the animals look like!"

Eva opened her backpack. "We have tape in the first-aid kit, and Mom always carries a sewing kit. I think we can repair the balloon."

Mr. Alvarez nodded. "Excellent!"

Hugo pointed. "Look, a giant Yucca tree. If we run out of food, we can eat its fruit!"

"You're very **resourceful**," said Mrs. Alvarez. "Keep thinking of things we may need in case we're here for a while."

Mrs. Alvarez and Eva made the repairs while Mr. Alvarez and Hugo looked for wood to build a fire.

"Dad, here is some dried Yucca. This wood is great for a fire," said Hugo.

The family sat around the fire and ate lunch. Soon, they heard a strange howl in the distance.

"It's time to get out of here," Mr. Alvarez declared.

The family quickly put out the fire got back in the air. Mr. Alvarez sighed with relief. He carefully steered the balloon away from the enormous plants.

"It looks like smooth sailing from here!" shouted Hugo.

GO ON →

Use "One Wild Ride!" to answer Numbers 1 through 5.

1 Read this paragraph from the passage.

> "It's hard to see!" shouted Mr. Alvarez. "This could be a serious problem. It's critical that I try to land the balloon."

Which word from the paragraph has about the same meaning as *critical*?

Ⓐ hard

Ⓑ serious

Ⓒ land

2 Which useful item does Eva pack that she uses to make the repair?

Ⓐ tape

Ⓑ a balloon

Ⓒ a sewing kit

3 Read this sentence from the passage.

> "You're very resourceful," said Mrs. Alvarez.

Which sentence from the passage gives a clue about the meaning of *resourceful*?

Ⓐ "If the plants are this big, I don't want to know what the animals look like!"

Ⓑ "Look, a giant Yucca tree."

Ⓒ "If we run out of food, we can eat its fruit!"

GO ON →

4 What does Hugo know about nature that is useful?

Ⓐ He knows where there is a safe place to land the balloon.

Ⓑ He knows to steer the balloon away from the large plants.

Ⓒ He knows that dried Yucca wood is good for starting a fire.

5 Which sentence best states the theme of the passage?

Ⓐ You can never be too prepared.

Ⓑ Emergencies can always be avoided.

Ⓒ Quick thinking can solve any problem.

GO ON →

Read "Patterns All Around You" before you answer Numbers 6 through 10.

Patterns All Around You

Step outside and look around. There are patterns all around you! Imagine being at the seashore. You gaze out toward the ocean and see big waves curling over and over again. Next, the waves flatten out and rush onto the sand. The water leaves behind a pattern in the sand. The pattern repeats itself, again and again. This is just one pattern in nature. What others have you seen?

Patterns in Nature

Think about a leaf that has fallen from a tree. You pick it up and study it. Its pattern is not **complex**. It is rather simple! If you cover half of the leaf, you can see it has a certain size and shape. It also has a series of veins. When you uncover the other half, you can see that it looks exactly like the part that you just studied! That is because both halves of the leaf are the same. They have the same size, shape, and vein markings.

You can see this in insects, as well. A butterfly has a similar kind of pattern as a leaf. Each butterfly wing is shaped the same. They also have the same colorful pattern. If you look closely, you can also see that there are antennae on each side.

A Spider's Web

Have you ever walked into a spider's web? This little critter is capable of building a complicated web during the night.

GO ON →

Think about the design of a spider's web. Some webs look like bicycle wheels. The spider builds a frame with its silk. Spokes, or rays of silk, are built from the center. They form a pattern. The spider sits in the center and waits to catch its prey. The spider senses another insect when it feels vibrations on its web. It rushes out and bites the other insect. This perfect web design is just another example of the amazing patterns we can discover in nature.

Diagram of a Beetle

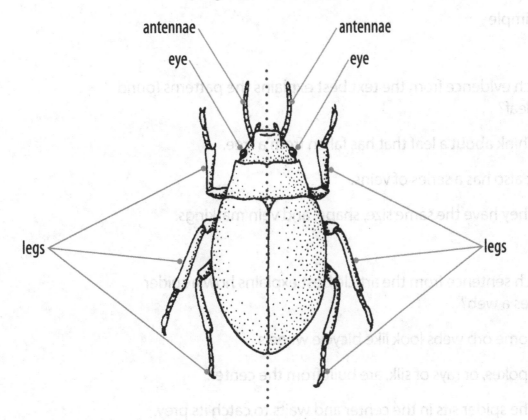

antennae   antennae
eye   eye
legs   legs

Use "Patterns All Around You" to answer Numbers 6 through 10.

6 Read these sentences from the article.

> You pick it up and study it. Its pattern is
> not complex. It is rather simple!

Which word from the sentences means the OPPOSITE
of *complex*?

Ⓐ study

Ⓑ pattern

Ⓒ simple

7 Which evidence from the text best explains the patterns found
in a leaf?

Ⓐ Think about a leaf that has fallen from a tree.

Ⓑ It also has a series of veins.

Ⓒ They have the same size, shape, and vein markings.

8 Which sentence from the article best explains how a spider
makes a web?

Ⓐ Some orb webs look like bicycle wheels.

Ⓑ Spokes, or rays of silk, are built from the center.

Ⓒ The spider sits in the center and waits to catch its prey.

GO ON →

9 What is the article mostly about?

Ⓐ patterns that are found in nature

Ⓑ patterns that waves make

Ⓒ patterns on insects

10 How does the diagram relate to the topic of the article?

Ⓐ It shows how the beetle looks the same on both sides.

Ⓑ It shows how the beetle can create new patterns.

Ⓒ It shows how the beetle has many legs.

Read "Tony Beaver, Lumberjack" before you answer Numbers 1 through 5.

Tony Beaver, Lumberjack

Long ago, there lived a family called the Beavers. There was Paw and Maw Beaver. They named their children Tony, Betsy, and Molly. The family had a tiny log cabin deep in the mountains of West Virginia.

Each day, Paw gave Tony a chore to do.

"Go on and chop down a tree. Maw needs some wood to build a fire."

Now, the one chore Tony enjoyed most was chopping trees. So, he picked up his ax and walked on a path to a wooded area. His little sisters tagged along. There, Tony chopped down a hickory tree. He did it with just a few mighty swings! After, he and his sisters hauled the wood back to the cabin.

One day, Tony went to the town of Turtle Cove. There, he spotted the best lumberjack around. His name was Big Bill Simpson. Big Bill was having a tree-chopping contest that day. He was giving an award for the mountaineer who could chop faster than him.

Tony loved the idea of contests. So, he decided to enter. When his name was called, he **sauntered** over to an ax and then strolled to the tree.

Big Bill shouted, "On your mark, get set, chop!"

Whack, whack, whack! Tony got into a fast-paced rhythm. It was like the beat of a drum. He was so fast that he chopped that ol' hickory tree into matchsticks! It only took him a minute! He won the contest easily.

GO ON →

From that day forward, Tony never stopped chopping down trees. Soon, he started his own lumberjack business along the banks of the Eel River.

Over time, Tony perfected his skills. He was known as the best lumberjack in the land. Tony's fame **entitled** him, or gave him the right, to be proud. He definitely deserved it!

People were amazed that he could chop down so many trees so fast. On the back swing, he cut down the tree behind him. On the down swing, he chopped down the tree in front of him. When Tony got bored, he set his ax down. With one mighty yank, he pulled out a tree by its roots!

Even to this day, Tony Beaver is famous. He is the best mountaineer to ever live in the hills of West Virginia.

GO ON →

Use "Tony Beaver, Lumberjack" to answer Numbers 1 through 5.

1 Who is the narrator of the passage?

Ⓐ a narrator who is not part of the story

Ⓑ Tony Beaver's sister

Ⓒ Big Bill Simpson

2 What does Tony Beaver think about chopping wood?

Ⓐ It is an enjoyable way to spend time.

Ⓑ It is a difficult and boring task.

Ⓒ It is a necessary chore.

3 Read this sentence from the passage.

**When his name was called, he sauntered over to an ax
and then strolled to the tree.**

Which clue word in the sentence helps explain what
saunutered means?

Ⓐ called

Ⓑ name

Ⓒ strolled

GO ON →

4 Which sentence from the passage best explains how the narrator feels about Tony?

Ⓐ From that day forward, Tony never stopped chopping down trees.

Ⓑ On the back swing, he cut down the tree behind him.

Ⓒ He is the best mountaineer to ever live in the hills of West Virginia.

5 Read this paragraph from the passage.

> **Over time, Tony perfected his skills. He was known as the best lumberjack in the land. Tony's fame entitled him, or gave him the right, to be proud. He definitely deserved it!**

Which phrase from the paragraph has about the same meaning as *entitled*?

Ⓐ perfected his skills

Ⓑ gave him the right

Ⓒ he definitely

Read "Shirin Ebadi and the Fight for Human Rights" before you answer Numbers 6 through 10.

Shirin Ebadi and the Fight for Human Rights

Shirin Ebadi is a gifted teacher and lawyer. She fights peacefully to help gain rights for women and children. She is also very courageous. At times, she has spoken out against the government where she used to live.

Early Life and Career

Shirin was born in the country of Iran in 1947. She was raised in the capital city of Tehran. In 1969, she received a law degree from the University of Tehran. Later, she became the first woman judge in Iran. This was a great accomplishment, for in her country, women do not have the same rights as men. She also became president of the city court in Tehran in 1975.

Shirin's life took a big turn four years later. During this time, Iran experienced a revolution. People with strong views took control of the country. Shirin was forced to step down as judge. She was denied her rights. Then she was offered a lower position. Instead of taking the job, she left her job. This determined woman would not **reconsider**, or revisit, her decision. She would not be a clerk in a court where she had once ruled as a judge.

Shirin tried to practice law, but it was not possible. Her application for a license was turned down. She began to write books about what she believed in. She wrote about human rights. She described the importance of freedom for everyone.

GO ON →

Peace and Rights for All

In 2003, Shirin was awarded the Nobel Peace Prize. This was a very high honor. It recognized her efforts in helping to gain rights for women and children.

Shirin is a founder of the Association for Support of Children's Rights in Iran. She also teaches at a university. Shirin leads training courses in human rights. She travels around the world to speak about it. Shirin is a role model and an inspiration to others. She is a fearless person who will help make the world a better place for women and children.

Any person who pursues human rights in Iran must live with fear...but I have learned to overcome my fear.

—Shirin Ebadi

GO ON →

Use "Shirin Ebadi and the Fight for Human Rights" to answer Numbers 6 through 10.

6 What evidence from the text does the author use to support the point of view that Shirin is courageous?

Ⓐ Shirin Ebadi is a gifted teacher and lawyer.

Ⓑ At times, she has spoken out against the government where she used to live.

Ⓒ Shirin tried to practice law, but it was not possible.

7 Read this sentence from the article.

> **This determined young woman would not reconsider, or revisit, her decision.**

Which clue word from the sentence helps to explain what *reconsider* means?

Ⓐ determined

Ⓑ revisit

Ⓒ decision

8 What does the author think of Shirin's decision to not accept a clerk position?

Ⓐ She was lucky.

Ⓑ She was stubborn.

Ⓒ She was determined.

9 With which statement would the author most likely agree?

Ⓐ Shirin's greatest accomplishment was becoming a judge.

Ⓑ Shirin's work inspires women and children everywhere.

Ⓒ Shirin's life has been a constant struggle.

10 The quote at the end of the article supports the author's point of view that Shirin is _____.

Ⓐ brave

Ⓑ hardworking

Ⓒ respected

STOP

Read "Life in Plymouth Colony" before you answer Numbers 1 through 5.

Life in Plymouth Colony

Dear Diary,

*I have just a moment to write this morning. It has been a difficult **transition** since we sailed from England four years ago. The change was very hard at first. We had little food, but now, life is good. We have plentiful food and a small, but cozy home. It reminds me of our home back in England because it, too, is made of timber and the roof is steeply pitched. There are still little reminders of our life in England. But oh, how I miss my friends!*

"Sarah! Samuel! It is time for chores," Mother called.

Sarah closed her diary and climbed down from the sleeping area. Then she picked up a pail and carried it to the stream to fetch water. When she returned, Sarah gathered wood from the shed and then helped her mother prepare a simple meal of porridge, corn bread, and cheese.

"Mother, don't you miss the market? We bought such wonderful foods there!" Sarah had a dreamy expression on her face.

"I do miss the market *and* our home, but life in the colony has been good to us."

"How?" asked Sarah.

"Our new friends are very **supportive**. We help each other and give each other strength. We are very lucky to have them."

"But don't we work much harder here?"

GO ON →

Mid-Unit Assessment · Unit 5

"Yes, that is for sure. You and your brother, Samuel, would be attending school now. Instead, he is out hunting with your father. Hopefully, they will bring back a bird for supper. Now, we must finish cooking. We have many chores left to do!"

After breakfast, Sarah and her mother cleaned their home. They stuffed their mattresses with straw. It was left over from the rye seed that Father and Samuel planted in the fields. Next, they made soap and then picked carrots and turnips from their garden.

Later that evening, Sarah helped Mother prepare supper, a simple stew made of duck and vegetables. Afterwards, Sarah and Samuel practiced their reading and writing. Their parents wanted them to take time each day to study. When they were done, the children played a game.

"Samuel, get the knicker box and marbles!" called Sarah. "Maybe tomorrow, we can get the other children to run races with us!"

"That is a fine idea," responded Mother. "You see, there is still time for fun even after a good day's work!"

GO ON →

Name: _____ **Date:** _____

Use "Life in Plymouth Colony" to answer Numbers 1 through 5.

1 Read this sentence from the passage.

> **It has been a difficult transition since we sailed from England four years ago.**

Which word from the passage has about the same meaning as *transition*?

Ⓐ moment

Ⓑ change

Ⓒ plentiful

2 How has life changed for Sarah and her family since first moving to the colony?

Ⓐ They did not have a big home, but now they do.

Ⓑ They did not have much food, but now they do.

Ⓒ They did not have friends, but now they do.

3 How is Sarah's home in the colony similar to her home in England?

Ⓐ It is about the same size.

Ⓑ It is next to a stream.

Ⓒ It is made of timber.

4 Read this sentence from the passage.

"**Our new friends are very supportive.**"

Which sentence from the passage gives a clue about the meaning of *supportive*?

Ⓐ "We help each other and give each other strength."

Ⓑ "We are very lucky to have them."

Ⓒ "We have many chores left to do!"

5 What is an example of something the family could do in both England and the colony?

Ⓐ go to the market

Ⓑ attend school

Ⓒ play games

Read "Invasion of the Asian Carp" before you answer Numbers 6 through 10.

Invasion of the Asian Carp

Imagine fishing off a boat on a warm, summer day. Suddenly, something flies out of the water. It is a fish! Soon, dozens of fish are leaping out of the water. They look as if they are flying. You duck down! What you are seeing is an invasion of a fish called silver carp. It is a type of Asian carp.

Escaping Up the Mississippi

In the 1970s, different kinds of carp were brought to the United States. These **variations** came from Southeast Asia. Asian carp include bighead, silver, grass, and black carp. People put the carp in commercial fishponds and waste treatment plants. The carp were used to remove algae in the ponds and sealed off areas.

But the carp escaped during floods and swam up the Mississippi River. Today, Asian carp are found in 18 states along the river! They are getting close to the Great Lakes region of the United States.

Upsetting the Balance

Many types of carp feed at the bottom of lakes and rivers. Asian carp are different. They feed toward the top of the water. They eat small organisms there. They eat the same food that other fish eat. And they eat a lot! Asian carp can eat about 20% of their body weight every day.

GO ON →

Unlike other kinds of fish, Asian carp are aggressive. They also grow fast. Silver carp jump out of the water when they are surprised. This can hurt people in boats. Bighead carp grow to be up to four feet long and weigh about 100 pounds! They take up a lot of space that other fish need to live.

Preventing Migration

Efforts are being made to stop Asian carp from entering the Great Lakes area. Electrical barriers have been built, but Asian carp are strong swimmers. If there is an opening, they may find a way through.

Use "Invasion of the Asian Carp" to answer Numbers 6 through 10.

6 What evidence from the text tells how the silver carp is different from other types of fish?

Ⓐ It is very large.

Ⓑ It is silver in color.

Ⓒ It flies out of the water.

7 Which word from the article has about the same meaning as *variations*?

Ⓐ kinds

Ⓑ include

Ⓒ treatment

8 How are the feeding habits of Asian carp different from other types of carp?

Ⓐ Asian carp feed only on plants.

Ⓑ Asian carp feed at the top of the water.

Ⓒ Asian carp feed less than other types of carp.

GO ON →

9 How are bighead carp different from silver carp?

Ⓐ Bighead carp are a type of Asian carp.

Ⓑ Bighead carp can grow to be very large.

Ⓒ Bighead carp swam up the Mississippi River.

10 According to the graph, which kind of Asian carp has become most common in the Mississippi River?

Ⓐ bighead carp

Ⓑ grass carp

Ⓒ silver carp

STOP

Read "Friends and Allies" before you answer Numbers 1 through 5.

Friends and Allies

Samantha and Keisha had been best friends for as long as they both could remember. The girls lived one block from the beach, so naturally, they grew up swimming and surfing together. Samantha and Keisha were going surfing today.

"Samantha, please wear your wetsuit!" yelled Mom from the kitchen. "The ocean temperature is very cold!"

"I know, I know," muttered Samantha. "It **insulates** me so that I don't lose body heat."

The girls carried their surfboards to the beach and waved hello to the lifeguard. They spent the afternoon catching waves, and when the water was calm, they rested in the sand.

"Are you ready for the swim team tryouts this week?" asked Samantha.

Keisha wondered aloud, asking, "What if one of us doesn't make the team?"

"No chance for that!" said Samantha confidently.

During tryouts, the girls cheered each other on. It was a long week because they wouldn't find out who made the team until Friday. After the final bell rang on Friday afternoon, they ran to the gym.

"We made it!" shouted Keisha, pointing at their names on the list.

"We have a swim meet on Monday, so we should practice tomorrow," said Samantha excitedly.

GO ON →

Keisha frowned. "I don't know how I feel about competing against you."

Samantha thought for a moment. "It will be okay. You're my **ally**, so we'll always be united, even when we race against each other!"

On Monday, the swim team rode the bus to the swim meet. The girls were in two races, one for each type of swim stroke: the butterfly and the freestyle. The first race was the butterfly. Keisha took a commanding lead, but toward the end, Sam started to pull ahead. When Keisha and Samantha reached for the pool wall, Samantha touched first!

For a moment, Keisha felt a pang of disappointment, but she recovered quickly. She was happy for her friend.

The next race was the freestyle. As soon as the race began, a swimmer from another school took the lead. By the end, Samantha and Keisha were neck-and-neck with her. The other swimmer touched first, Keisha was second, and Samantha was third.

"Great job!" Samantha shouted as she hugged her friend. "It does feel strange racing against each other, but it's a good thing because we get to practice together and help each other get better. What do you say we practice tomorrow?"

Keisha smiled. "That sounds like a great plan!"

GO ON →

Use "Friends and Allies" to answer Numbers 1 through 5.

1 Which sentence from the text gives a clue about the meaning of *insulates*?

Ⓐ swimming and surfing

Ⓑ the ocean temperature

Ⓒ so that I don't lose body heat

2 How does Samantha try to reassure Keisha about trying out for the swim team?

Ⓐ She tells her they will both make the team.

Ⓑ She tells her to practice before the tryouts.

Ⓒ She tells her they will always be friends.

3 Read these sentences from the passage.

> **Samantha thought for a moment. "It will be okay.
> You're my ally, so we'll always be united, even when
> we race against each other!"**

Which word from these sentences helps to explain the meaning of *ally*?

Ⓐ moment

Ⓑ united

Ⓒ race

GO ON →

4 What does Keisha do when she loses the butterfly race?

Ⓐ She becomes angry and upset.

Ⓑ She thinks it is good that her friend won.

Ⓒ She begins to worry that she is not a good swimmer.

5 Why does Samantha tell Keisha that it is a good thing to race against each other?

Ⓐ They can help each other improve.

Ⓑ They can take turns winning races.

Ⓒ They can teach each other to swim.

GO ON →

Read "California Sea Otters" before you answer Numbers 6 through 10.

California Sea Otters

Are you an otter spotter? If you ever visit California, be on the lookout. You just might spot a cute sea creature! It is called the California sea otter.

Sea Otter Features

The sea otter has the world's densest fur. It has one million hairs per square inch of its body. A sea otter needs a thick fur coat. It keeps the sea otter warm in cold waters. A sea otter spends a couple of hours each day grooming its coat. This keeps its fur healthy.

Sea otters eat a rich **diversity** of foods. They enjoy many different clams, crabs, and sea urchins. They also eat sea stars and snails. It can be fun to watch them eat. They lie on their backs, eating while they swim at the same time!

Sea Otters Struggle

Long ago, the California sea otter lived all along the Pacific coast. Today, there are fewer otter habitats. They struggle to survive. There are about 2,500 sea otters living in central California. Scientists are not sure why the population is not growing. Coastal pollution and oil spills may be causes. Both can harm the sea otter population.

GO ON →

The Monterey Bay Aquarium

The Monterey Bay Aquarium is a "must-visit" place. Here, scientists are exploring ways to save sea otters. They rescue injured otters and care for them. Scientists release them again when they are healthy. Sea otters stay at the aquarium if they are not healthy enough to return to the wild.

When you go there, be sure to visit the "Otter Spotter Station." You can talk with staff members. You can observe and monitor sea otters. You'll use a radio tracking device to track their movements. You will even use binoculars to get a good look at these interesting creatures!

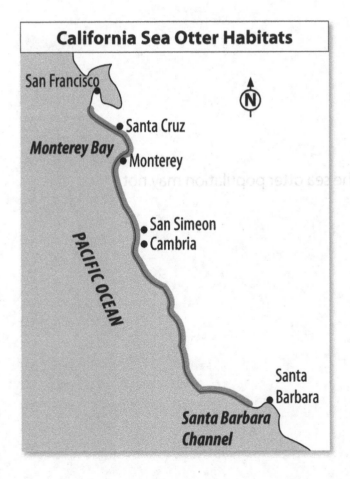

GO ON →

Use "California Sea Otters" to answer Numbers 6 through 10.

6 What causes a sea otter's fur to stay healthy?

Ⓐ swimming in the water

Ⓑ eating different foods

Ⓒ grooming each day

7 Read this sentence from the article.

Sea otters eat a rich diversity of foods.

Which words from the article have about the same meaning as *diversity*?

Ⓐ in cold waters

Ⓑ many different

Ⓒ same time

8 Which is NOT a reason why the sea otter population may not be growing?

Ⓐ lack of food to eat

Ⓑ coastal pollution

Ⓒ oil spills

GO ON →

Name: _____ **Date:** _____

9 Scientists at the Monterey Bay Aquarium rescue and care for injured sea otters to _____.

Ⓐ increase their population in Monterey

Ⓑ allow visitors to watch them and learn about them

Ⓒ make them healthy enough to send back into the wild

10 Based on the map, in which city would you likely spot a sea otter?

Ⓐ Santa Cruz

Ⓑ San Francisco

Ⓒ Santa Barbara

STOP

Unit
Assessment

Read "Ajay's Small Business" before you answer Numbers 1 through 7.

Ajay's Small Business

Ajay searched the garage one afternoon.

Dad grinned. "What are you looking for now, Ajay?"

"I saw an old mailbox the other day. I think I could turn it into a birdhouse!"

Dad laughed. "That's a creative idea. I never would have thought of that."

Dad found the mailbox. First, Ajay drew a sketch of what the birdhouse would look like. Next, he painted a colorful design on it. Then, Ajay attached an old metal chain to it. He hung the birdhouse on a tree in the front yard and put a small cup of birdseed inside.

The birds loved their new birdhouse. A few days later, a neighbor knocked at the door.

"Hi, Mr. Samuels. Are you looking for my dad?"

"No, son," he smiled. "I was wondering where you bought that birdhouse. It's a clever invention!"

"Why, I made it myself!" said Ajay proudly.

"My wife collects teapots," said Mr. Samuels. "If I gave you an old one, could you turn it into a birdhouse? I would pay you for it."

"I'd love to!" Ajay was thrilled. He could not wait to get started.

GO ON →

More neighbors heard about Ajay's birdhouses, and people came to his house every week. They asked him to make birdhouses using different things. Ajay used coffee cans and old pans and flowerpots. He even used **debris** from the yard, such as fallen branches and loose rocks.

Ajay used the **wages** that he earned to buy materials, and soon he had spent most of his earnings. He could not make the birdhouses fast enough, so he needed a new plan.

"Dad, do you think you could **loan** me some money?"

"I thought you were earning money. Why do you need to borrow more?" asked Dad.

"I'm using what I earn to buy materials. I need to borrow money to hire a friend who can help me build the birdhouses. We can put together more birdhouses faster."

"Great idea, Ajay!" said Dad with a smile. "Of course I will lend you the money."

Ajay and his friend Maya began building the birdhouses together. At the end of each week, Ajay paid Maya for her help. After a month, Ajay paid back the loan. He decided to put his extra earnings in the bank. He was not sure what he would do with the money yet, but he loved that his small business was growing!

GO ON →

Use "Ajay's Small Business" to answer Numbers 1 through 7.

1 What problem does Ajay solve at the beginning of the passage?

Ⓐ He finds a birdhouse in the garage.

Ⓑ He helps Mr. Samuels make a mailbox.

Ⓒ He turns an old mailbox into a birdhouse.

2 What happens right after Ajay builds a teapot birdhouse for his neighbor?

Ⓐ He makes more birdhouses for his neighbors.

Ⓑ He hangs a birdhouse on a tree in his front yard.

Ⓒ He puts money from selling birdhouses into the bank.

3 Read these sentences from the passage.

> They asked him to make birdhouses using different things. Ajay used coffee cans and old pans and flowerpots. He even used debris from the yard, such as fallen branches and loose rocks.

Which phrase from these sentences is an example of *debris*?

Ⓐ coffee cans

Ⓑ old pans

Ⓒ loose rocks

Copyright © McGraw-Hill Education. Permission is granted to reproduce for classroom use.

GO ON ➜

4 What problem does Ajay have while building birdhouses for others?

(A) He cannot build the birdhouses fast enough.

(B) He runs out of materials to make the birdhouses.

(C) He builds more birdhouses than he is able to sell.

5 Which word from the passage has the same meaning as *wages*?

(A) materials

(B) earnings

(C) birdhouses

6 Read this sentence from the passage.

   "Dad, do you think you could loan me some money?"

Which sentence from the passage helps you figure out the meaning of *loan*?

(A) "I thought you were earning money."

(B) "Why do you need to borrow more?" asked Dad.

(C) "I'm using what I earn to buy materials."

7 What does Ajay do after he pays back the loan?

(A) He pays Maya for her help.

(B) He builds all of the birdhouses.

(C) He puts his money in the bank.

Read "A Good Inventor" before you answer Numbers 8 through 15.

A Good Inventor

An Amazing Invention

It was a cold December day in 1873. Chester Greenwood was ice-skating on a pond in Farmington, Maine. He was 15 years old. Chester's ears were freezing. He decided to wrap them in a scarf. It was hard to skate wearing the itchy scarf. He knew he needed a better solution.

So, Chester decided to make his own ear protectors. First, he made ear-shaped loops. He used metal wire. Next, he covered the wire with beaver fur. His grandmother helped him sew on the fur. Later, he used a steel band to connect each loop. Chester placed the band over his head. *Ta-da!* His ears were now safe from the cold. He just needed one more thing. He added a velvet covering to make it soft. Now it was perfect!

An Idea Grows

People in Farmington loved Chester's invention. They all wanted their own ear protectors. Chester was excited. He knew that people could get government **patents** for their ideas. This would allow him to make and sell his ear protectors. Chester decided to get one. He received a patent in 1877.

After that, Chester formed a company. He called it Greenwood's Ear Protector Factory. The company was a smart idea. It began producing his invention. He hired people to work for him. He also put out some advertisements.

GO ON →

The Earmuff Capital of the World

Chester continued to improve his invention. He attached tiny hinges to each covering. This helped the ear protectors fit better and allowed him to fold them. Now they could be carried in a coat pocket.

Chester's factory made thousands of ear protectors. It even made ear protectors for American soldiers during World War I. Farmington became known as "The Earmuff Capital of the World"!

More Good Inventions

Chester did not stop there. He would soon **accomplish** much more. He succeeded in making other helpful inventions such as a folding bed and a steel-tooth rake. Chester went on to get patents for more than 100 inventions. Many of these inventions are still useful today.

GO ON →

Use "A Good Inventor" to answer Numbers 8 through 15.

8 Why did Chester invent ear protectors?

Ⓐ He needed to keep warm while ice-skating.

Ⓑ He did not have a scarf on a cold winter day.

Ⓒ He learned how to sew with his grandmother.

9 Chester added velvet covering to the ear protectors to make them _____.

Ⓐ safe

Ⓑ soft

Ⓒ warm

10 Read this sentence from the article.

> **He knew that people could get government patents for their ideas.**

Which sentence from the text gives a clue about the meaning of *patents*?

Ⓐ People in Farmington loved Chester's invention.

Ⓑ This would allow him to make and sell his ear protectors.

Ⓒ He called it Greenwood's Ear Protector Factory.

GO ON →

11 Which sentence from the article best states the author's point of view about Chester's company?

   Ⓐ The company was a smart idea.

   Ⓑ It began producing his invention.

   Ⓒ He also put out some advertisements.

12 Which section of the article tells how Chester made his invention better?

   Ⓐ An Amazing Invention

   Ⓑ An Idea Grows

   Ⓒ The Earmuff Capital of the World

13 Why did Chester add hinges to his ear protectors?

   Ⓐ so they could be folded up

   Ⓑ so American soldiers could use them

   Ⓒ so the factory could produce more of them

GO ON →

14 Read these sentences from the article.

> **He would soon accomplish much more. He succeeded in making other helpful inventions such as a folding bed and a steel-tooth rake.**

Which clue word in the sentences helps to explain what *accomplish* means?

Ⓐ succeeded

Ⓑ making

Ⓒ helpful

15 Which sentence from the article best states the author's point of view about Chester's overall success?

Ⓐ He hired people to work for him.

Ⓑ Chester continued to improve his invention.

Ⓒ Many of these inventions are still useful today.

STOP

Read "Good Luck Can Lie in a Button" before you answer Numbers 1 through 8.

Good Luck Can Lie in a Button

Everyone will have good luck at least once in a lifetime. This is a tale about one man who found good luck in an unexpected place!

Once upon a time, there lived a poor man. His job was making umbrella fasteners. But the money he earned only paid for his daily food.

As he worked, day in and day out, he mumbled to himself, "I do not have good luck. I can never find good luck."

The man did not know that good luck could be found in a pear tree. The pear tree was sitting in his back yard. But the tree would bear no fruit.

One night, the state of his life changed. His **circumstances** would never be the same again. At midnight, there was a terrible storm. A large branch broke from the pear tree. In the morning, the man brought the branch to his workshop. As a joke, he carved tiny wooden pears out of the branch.

"Now this tree has pears!" he grinned. He handed out the wooden pears to children. Then, he watched as they played with them. This made the man happy for a short time. But soon he forgot about the wooden pears.

One day, it began to rain. He used his umbrella to get from his house to the workshop. It was so windy that the umbrella turned inside out! When he got to his workshop, he tried to fix it. But he lost the fastener that tied it together. He searched and searched for it. Then he saw a tiny wooden pear on the floor.

GO ON →

"This will do!" he said to himself. So he cut a hole in it and pulled a string through it. The man was very pleased with the **outcome**, or result, of his idea. "This is the best fastener my umbrella has ever had!"

The man sold his umbrellas around the countryside. Soon, people noticed that the little pears were better fasteners than the old buttons. They wanted umbrellas with little pears as buttons!

The man wanted to make the best umbrella buttons in the land. He **shuddered** with the unhappy thought that someone else would do a better job than him. Soon, he cut up the entire pear tree to make pear buttons. With his money, he built a large workshop. He hired workers to help him. Now the man enjoyed great happiness all of the time. He often thought to himself: "Good luck can lie in a button!"

Use "Good Luck Can Lie in a Button" to answer Numbers 1 through 8.

1 What is the message in the first paragraph?

Ⓐ People will find good luck even if they have no money.

Ⓑ People will find good luck at least once in their lives.

Ⓒ People will find good luck if they look for it.

2 How does the man feel at the beginning of the passage?

Ⓐ He is sad because he is always hungry.

Ⓑ He is upset because nothing good happens to him.

Ⓒ He is angry because his pear tree does not grow fruit.

GO ON →

3 Read these sentences from the passage.

> **One night, the state of his life changed. His circumstances would never be the same again. At midnight, there was a terrible storm.**

Which words from the sentences have about the same meaning as *circumstances*?

Ⓐ state of his life

Ⓑ the same again

Ⓒ terrible storm

4 Compared to the original fasteners, the wooden pear buttons _____.

Ⓐ are larger

Ⓑ cost more

Ⓒ work better

5 Read this sentence from the passage.

> **The man was very pleased with the outcome, or result, of his idea.**

Which clue word from the passage tells the meaning of *outcome*?

Ⓐ pleased

Ⓑ result

Ⓒ idea

GO ON →

Name: _____ **Date:** _____

6 How does the man change after he finds the broken pear branch?

Ⓐ He becomes happier.

Ⓑ He becomes smarter.

Ⓒ He becomes better at his job.

7 Read these sentences from the passage.

> The man wanted to make the best umbrella buttons in the land. He shuddered with the unhappy thought that someone else would do a better job than him.

Which phrase from the sentences gives a clue about the meaning of *shuddered*?

Ⓐ best umbrella

Ⓑ unhappy thought

Ⓒ better job

8 What is the main message of the passage?

Ⓐ You can find good luck even when you do not expect to.

Ⓑ You can find good luck when you make money.

Ⓒ You can find good luck when you grow a tree.

GO ON →

Read "The United Nations" before you answer Numbers 9 through 15.

The United Nations

The United Nations Is Born

In 1941, the leaders of the United States and Great Britain held a meeting. They were concerned about world security. The leaders wanted to make sure that countries were safe. They worked together to write the Atlantic Charter. This statement explained goals that would help them keep peace and safety in the world. They hoped for a better future for all.

In 1942, 26 nations met in Washington, D.C. They all signed a pledge. It was called the Declaration by United Nations. They were now joined together as allies.

The allies stood against the threats of Germany, Italy, and Japan. They fought against these countries in World War II. On October 24, 1945, the United Nations was created. United Nations Day is celebrated every year on October 24th.

How the United Nation Works

The United Nations (UN) invites peaceful countries to join. Today, there are 193 countries in the United Nations. They make up a group called the General Assembly.

The countries have **representatives**. These members vote each time a decision is made. It does not matter whether a country is rich or poor, big or small. Each country gets one vote.

GO ON →

In Search of Peace

The General Assembly tries to **resolve** problems by using peaceful ways to fix things. But it cannot make laws. It helps countries where there is conflict. The UN also has inspection teams. These teams go to countries to look for weapons. They shut down places that make dangerous weapons.

The UN solves other problems, too. If there is a war or disaster, it sends aid. Workers provide water, food, and supplies. The UN also speaks out for human rights. Some of its goals are to get rid of disease and poor living conditions. The UN is an important group that helps many people.

A History of the United Nations

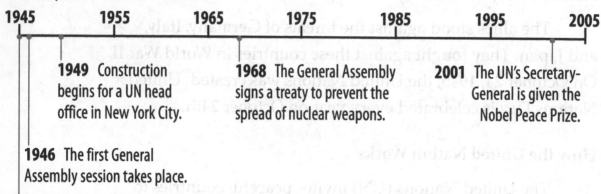

1945   1955   1965   1975   1985   1995   2005

1949 Construction begins for a UN head office in New York City.

1968 The General Assembly signs a treaty to prevent the spread of nuclear weapons.

2001 The UN's Secretary-General is given the Nobel Peace Prize.

1946 The first General Assembly session takes place.

1945 The United Nations is born with 51 countries.

GO ON →

Use "The United Nations" to answer Numbers 9 through 15.

9 What problem did the United States and Great Britain meet to discuss?

Ⓐ There were threats against the allies.

Ⓑ There was concern about world security.

Ⓒ There was conflict over the Atlantic Charter.

10 Which event happened first?

Ⓐ The United Nations was born.

Ⓑ The Atlantic Charter was written.

Ⓒ The Declaration by United Nations was signed.

11 What evidence from the article tells what happened right after the Declaration by United Nations was signed?

Ⓐ The allies stood against the threats of Germany, Italy, and Japan.

Ⓑ In 1942, 26 nations met in Washington, D.C.

Ⓒ United Nations Day is celebrated every year on October 24th.

GO ON →

12 Read this sentence from the article.

The countries have representatives.

Which word from the article has about the SAME meaning as *representatives*?

Ⓐ goals

Ⓑ countries

Ⓒ members

13 What actions does the United Nations take to try to solve problems?

Ⓐ It sends aid if there is a war or disaster.

Ⓑ It has inspection teams for its workers.

Ⓒ It makes laws against dangerous weapons.

14 Read this sentence from the article.

The General Assembly tries to resolve problems by using peaceful ways to fix things.

Which clue word helps to explain what *resolve* means?

Ⓐ tries

Ⓑ using

Ⓒ fix

GO ON →

15 According to the time line, in what year did the first General Assembly session take place?

Ⓐ 1945

Ⓑ 1946

Ⓒ 1949

Read "The Magic Carpet" before you answer Numbers 1 through 7.

The Magic Carpet

Ling and her mother were on a flight to Beijing, China, to visit Ling's grandmother. Ling was excited to see Popo again, but she was also excited to miss Chinese school at home. Her mother made her go every Saturday to learn **cultural** traditions and other things about Chinese life. Mother always said, "We must remember our roots."

Ling watched movies during the flight. Then, she zipped up her red sweater and fell asleep. When she opened her eyes, the plane was pulling up to the airport. They collected their luggage and took a taxi to her grandmother's home.

"Popo!" cried Ling when her grandmother opened the door.

"Welcome!" said her grandmother. "You have grown so much!"

The family spent the day catching up. That night, Ling's mother went to bed early, but Ling and her grandmother sat up talking.

"Do you like Chinese school?" asked her grandmother.

"Not really. I don't see why I need to learn so much about Chinese culture."

Ling's grandmother took down a carpet hanging on the wall, and she placed it on the floor. It looked very old and had a beautiful dragon design on it.

"This carpet belonged to *my* grandmother," she explained. "Sit down and close your eyes."

GO ON →

Ling looked puzzled, but she did as she was told. Seconds later, she opened her eyes. They were flying through the air on the magical dragon carpet! The city of Beijing stretched out for miles before them.

"Look, Ling. There's the Forbidden City. Long ago, the emperor lived there."

"Why are so many buildings and signs red?" Ling asked. "Mother always wants me to wear red."

"Red stands for good luck."

Ling pointed and asked, "What's that place?"

"It's called Tiananmen Square. I can take you there tomorrow to do Tai Chi and fly kites."

"I love flying kites, but Tai Chi not so much. Mother wants me to practice," frowned Ling.

"It is a traditional exercise that is good for your health."

Ling suddenly gasped. "Wow, that building looks like a giant bird's nest!"

Her grandmother laughed. "It's the National Stadium. That is where the 2008 Olympics were held."

Ling gazed in wonder. "It reminds me of the bird's nest soup mother makes. She uses noodles and shapes them into a nest. Mother teaches me Chinese cooking. I will make spring rolls and sticky rice cakes tomorrow!"

"I would love that, Ling! Your mother's teachings will make sure our family's culture is **preserved** so that it won't be lost or forgotten. Now let's head home and get some rest."

Ling smiled. Suddenly, Chinese school didn't seem so bad.

GO ON →

Use "The Magic Carpet" to answer Numbers 1 through 7.

1 What evidence from the text gives a clue about the meaning of *cultural*?

Ⓐ things about Chinese life

Ⓑ movies during the flight

Ⓒ a taxi to her grandmother's home

2 How does Ling feel about Chinese school before going to visit her grandmother?

Ⓐ Ling is excited about going to Chinese school.

Ⓑ Ling will miss Chinese school when it is over.

Ⓒ Ling does not like going to Chinese school.

3 Why does Ling's mother want her to wear red?

Ⓐ Ling's grandmother always wears red.

Ⓑ Red is a popular color in Beijing, China.

Ⓒ In Chinese culture, red stands for good luck.

4 What traditional Chinese activity does Ling do only because her mother wants her to?

Ⓐ flying kites

Ⓑ practicing Tai Chi

Ⓒ visiting National Stadium

5 What does the National Stadium remind Ling of?

Ⓐ a dish that her mother makes

Ⓑ her Chinese school back home

Ⓒ her grandmother's magic carpet

6 Read this paragraph from the passage.

> "I would love that, Ling! Your mother's teachings
> will make sure our family culture is preserved so that
> it won't be lost or forgotten. Now let's head home and
> get some rest."

Which word from the paragraph means the OPPOSITE
of *preserved*?

Ⓐ love

Ⓑ lost

Ⓒ rest

7 Which sentence best states the theme of the passage?

Ⓐ Visiting with family helps us remember our past.

Ⓑ Going to school can teach us the traditions of our culture.

Ⓒ Understanding the importance of culture helps us to keep
it alive.

GO ON →

Read "Firefighters to the Rescue" before you answer Numbers 8 through 15.

Firefighters to the Rescue

Firefighters are very brave. They perform difficult and sometimes dangerous work. They provide services that are important to keep our communities safe. Fire departments put out millions of fires every year. These fires often involve large **structures**, such as houses. They can also include forests, cars or trucks, and even trash.

Teamwork

There is a lot of teamwork that goes into fighting fires. Each member of the crew counts on one another for help and support. Firefighters work together to get the job done.

Many pieces of equipment have to be handled when putting out a fire. Firefighters work together to do safety checks. They make sure the equipment **functions** properly. They need it to work correctly.

Sometimes, firefighters work with a partner when they put out fires. This helps to keep them safe. The partners look out for each other. For example, a firefighter would never enter a burning building alone.

Fire chiefs and officers work hard every day. They are responsible for their crews. They decide the best way to put out a fire quickly and safely. They also check that there is not a **shortage** of water before going to the scene of a fire. Having enough water is necessary and very important.

GO ON →

Fire Safety

Besides the fire department, other groups teach people about fire safety. One group is called the National Fire Protection Association. Its website lists building and electrical rules. These rules must be followed by schools, builders, and other groups. There are fact sheets on the website, too. This information teaches people how to avoid fire accidents at home.

Doing Your Part

How can you do your part? Practice fire safety when you are at school. Know where the exits with lighted signs are. Then you will know how to get out in case there is a fire. Take fire drills seriously. Stay calm if an alarm sounds. Leave your classroom quickly. And always follow your teacher's directions.

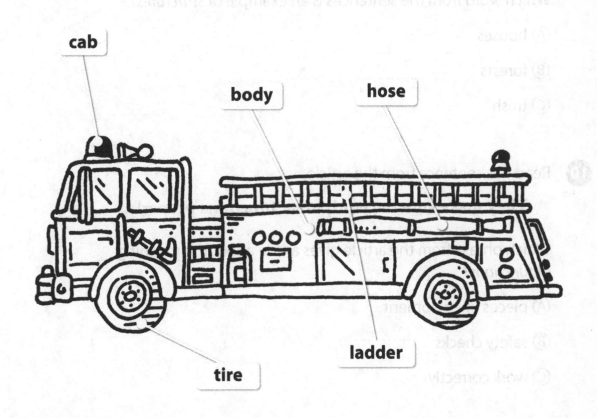

cab
body
hose
ladder
tire

GO ON →

Use "Firefighters to the Rescue" to answer Numbers 8 through 15.

8 Which sentence from the article supports the author's point of view that firefighters are brave?

Ⓐ They perform difficult and sometimes dangerous work.

Ⓑ They provide services that are important to keep our communities safe.

Ⓒ Firefighters work together to get the job done.

9 Read these sentences from the article.

> **These fires often involve large structures, such as houses. They can also include forests, cars or trucks, and even trash.**

Which word from the sentences is an example of *structures?*

Ⓐ houses

Ⓑ forests

Ⓒ trash

10 Read this sentence from the article.

> **They make sure the equipment functions properly.**

Which phrase from the article gives a clue about the meaning of *functions?*

Ⓐ pieces of equipment

Ⓑ safety checks

Ⓒ work correctly

GO ON →

Unit Assessment · Unit 3

11 Which sentence states the author's point of view about fire chiefs and officers?

Ⓐ They work harder than firefighters.

Ⓑ They have a lot of responsibility.

Ⓒ They make excellent partners.

12 Read this sentence from the article.

> They also check that there is not a shortage of water before going to the scene of a fire.

Which phrase from the article means the OPPOSITE of *shortage*?

Ⓐ work hard

Ⓑ quickly and safely

Ⓒ having enough

13 What is the main topic of the last paragraph?

Ⓐ fire safety in schools

Ⓑ fire safety in organizations

Ⓒ fire safety in the community

GO ON →

14 Which detail from the article explains a way that you can do your part to practice fire safety?

Ⓐ Fire departments put out millions of fires every year.

Ⓑ One group is called the National Fire Protection Association.

Ⓒ Know where the exits with lighted signs are.

15 According to the diagram, where is the cab located on the fire truck?

Ⓐ in front of the body

Ⓑ below the ladder

Ⓒ behind the hose

STOP

Read "The Drought Buster" before you answer Numbers 1 through 7.

The Drought Buster

This here story is about the greatest drought buster who ever lived. He could break even the driest drought. Whoa, now! I'm gettin' ahead of myself. Let's start from the beginning....

In the early days, when folks called settlers were settling the Great Plains, there was a drought. The fields were **barren**. Not a single corn stalk could be found in miles. One summer, it was particularly hot. The sun scorched the fields until they turned brown. Wispy, white clouds passed over quickly, but did nothing to block the harsh sun. Not a single drop of rain fell that summer.

Febold Feboldson, the famous Swedish drought buster, was frustrated. He wanted to go fishing, but there were no fish to be caught in the heat. Febold got so annoyed that he decided to do something drastic.

"I'm goin' to bust up this drought!" he muttered to himself. And that's just what the mighty plainsman did!

Febold got out his trusty ax. With just a couple of swings, he chopped down ten large trees. In a matter of seconds, Febold split the logs into smaller pieces of wood. Then he hauled that wood to the lake. In just one hour, he had built bonfires around the entire lake.

When the bonfires got good and hot, the water started to evaporate. It changed from a liquid to a gas until it disappeared altogether. Huge clouds started to form. The clouds got so big that they blotted out the sun. Soon, they were bumping into each other, and all that bumping made the rain come. Whoa, did it come! Soon it was raining cats and dogs.

GO ON →

Name: _____ Date: _____

Febold gazed up at the sky and laughed. He was proud that he busted up another drought. When he got home that night, he was soaking wet. He took off his shirt to **wring** it out. He squeezed the water out of that shirt and filled up an entire barrel!

Febold, the amazing drought buster, was happy. But the settlers on the plains had a different opinion. They were pleased their crops would grow again, but they grumbled because now they had no place to swim!

Use "The Drought Buster" to answer Numbers 1 through 7.

1 Who is the narrator of the passage?

Ⓐ Febold Feboldson

Ⓑ a settler on the plains

Ⓒ a speaker outside the story

2 Read this sentence from the passage.

The fields were barren.

Which sentence from the passage gives a clue about the meaning of *barren*?

Ⓐ Not a single corn stalk could be found in miles.

Ⓑ One summer, it was particularly hot.

Ⓒ The sun scorched the fields until they turned brown.

GO ON →

3 Which evidence from the text best supports the narrator's point of view that Febold is mighty?

Ⓐ Febold Feboldson, the famous Swedish drought buster, was frustrated.

Ⓑ With just a couple of swings, he chopped down ten large trees.

Ⓒ He squeezed the water out of that shirt and filled up an entire barrel!

4 Which detail from the text is exaggerated to give you a clue that this passage is a tall tale?

Ⓐ Febold got so annoyed that he decided to do something drastic.

Ⓑ In a matter of seconds, Febold split the logs into smaller pieces of wood.

Ⓒ It changed from a liquid to a gas until it disappeared altogether.

5 What lesson could be learned from the tall tale?

Ⓐ Never give up hope in rough times.

Ⓑ Some people are luckier than others.

Ⓒ You can never please everyone in life.

GO ON →

6 Read this sentence from the passage.

> **He took off his shirt to wring it out.**

Which word from the passage has about the same meaning as *wring*?

Ⓐ soaking

Ⓑ squeezed

Ⓒ filled

7 What does Febold think of his actions at the end of the passage?

Ⓐ He is proud of what he has done.

Ⓑ He is unsure of what will happen next.

Ⓒ He is excited to find a new place to swim.

GO ON →

Read "César Chávez: Labor Leader" before you answer Numbers 8 through 15.

César Chávez: Labor Leader

César Chávez started the first successful U.S. agricultural union. He formed this group to help improve conditions for farm workers. César would dedicate his life to improving the lives of others. Here is his story.

Life as a Migrant Worker

César was born near Yuma, Arizona, on March 31, 1927. He was one of six children. He lived a comfortable life with his family on their ranch. However, when the Great Depression happened, César's father could not pay taxes on his ranch. The family had to move. César's family, like hundreds of others, went to California. They hoped to find work there.

The Chávez family began working as migrant laborers. During harvest time, they traveled to different farms across the state. They picked fruits and vegetables.

César attended more than 30 different schools because his family moved so often. He left school when he was just 15 years old. César struggled as a full-time migrant laborer. In his spare time, he wanted to learn so that he could improve the quality of his life.

César was **inquisitive** about different world leaders. He was curious to find out how they used their influence to help others. This was a sign of things to come in César's own life.

GO ON →

Leader and Activist

When César grew up, he was concerned about the working conditions of migrant laborers. He knew first-hand what it was like to work long, difficult hours outdoors. César began working at the Community Service Organization (CSO). There, he helped other Hispanic Americans. In 1962, he founded the National Farm Workers Association (NFWA). This group **sought** to improve working conditions for migrant workers. César looked for ways to get health benefits for workers. They needed higher wages, too. César tried to make a change peacefully. He led protests and marches to reach his goals.

In 1972, the NFWA became the United Farm Workers of America (UFW). César served as its president until his death in 1993. His hard work and dedication would **affect** and influence millions of people during his lifetime.

In His Own Words – Quotes by César Chávez

About Migrant Workers	"If you really want to make a friend, go to someone's house and eat with him…. The people who give you their food give you their heart."
About Change	"Once social change begins, it cannot be reversed. You cannot uneducate the person who has learned to read."
About Unions	"We believe that unions have always been about much more than the industries they operate. The fight is never about grapes or lettuce….It is always about people."

GO ON →

Name: _____ Date: _____

Use "César Chávez: Labor Leader" to answer Numbers 8 through 15.

8 Based on the article, what does the author think of the daily life of migrant workers?

Ⓐ They earned enough money during harvest to live a comfortable life.

Ⓑ They ate well because there were so many fresh fruits and vegetables.

Ⓒ They faced difficulties because they had to move around so often.

9 Read these sentences from the article.

> César was inquisitive about different world leaders. He was curious to find out how they used their influence to help others.

Which word from the sentences has almost the same meaning as *inquisitive*?

Ⓐ different

Ⓑ world

Ⓒ curious

10 Based on the article, what is the author's point of view of César as a leader?

Ⓐ He thought of others and tried to do what was best for them.

Ⓑ He did not care if some people did not want to follow him.

Ⓒ He worked hard but needed a lot of support from others.

GO ON →

11 How does the author show how César tried to make a change?

Ⓐ by telling about protests and marches he led

Ⓑ by giving the names of large organizations

Ⓒ by describing his interest in world leaders

12 Read these sentences from the article.

> In 1962, he founded the National Farm Workers Association (NFWA). This group sought to improve working conditions for migrant workers.

Which words from the article have a similar meaning to the word *sought*?

Ⓐ began working at

Ⓑ looked for ways

Ⓒ make a change

13 Read these sentences from the article.

> César served as its president until his death in 1993. His hard work and dedication would affect and make a difference for millions of people during his lifetime.

Which phrase from the sentences helps to explain the meaning of *affect*?

Ⓐ served as its president

Ⓑ make a difference

Ⓒ during his lifetime

GO ON →

14 What evidence from the text best supports the author's point of view that César understood migrant workers?

Ⓐ He knew first-hand what it was like to work long, difficult hours outdoors.

Ⓑ César began working at the Community Service Organization (CSO).

Ⓒ César tried to make a change peacefully.

15 Based on the chart, what do all of César's quotes have in common?

Ⓐ They are about the importance of change.

Ⓑ They are about the importance of unions.

Ⓒ They are about the importance of people.

Read "Westward Ho!" before you answer Numbers 1 through 7.

Westward Ho!

Mary Bond sat in the back of the covered wagon and began to write in her diary.

Today is Tuesday. Sometimes it is hard to remember what day it is! I wonder what Oregon will be like when we finally get there.

We have been traveling for more than three months now. The countryside is so different from New York City! The pastures are green and the streams sparkle with clear water. It is not noisy like the city, and we have not seen one building in miles!

I believe that my **perspective** *and view of the wilderness is changing. I think I shall like living in the country, after all.*

"Mary, step down from the wagon!" shouted Father. "Why don't you walk alongside the wagon with your brother?"

Mary sighed and closed her diary. Then, she stepped off the wagon and ran to catch up with Stewart.

"When do you think we'll get to Oregon?" her younger brother asked.

"It may take us a couple more months," replied Mary.

"Don't you miss eating dessert every night?" asked Stewart seriously.

Mary laughed. "I mostly miss fresh fruits and vegetables—and different kinds of meat! I'm a bit tired of eating rice, dried meat, and dried fruit. It will be nice when we can grow our own fruits and vegetables. We can raise our own chickens, too!"

GO ON →

That night, the Bond family sat around the campfire.

"Father, what will we do first when we get to Oregon?" asked Mary.

"We will buy land. I hear it costs $2.00 an acre."

Mother replied, "Before that, we will look for a big piece of land, much larger than our yard in the city! We hope to find a nice plot of land along a river so that we will have a fresh supply of water…"

"And fish!" Stewart finished his mother's sentence.

Father added, "It will be good to **rely** and depend upon our land to grow our food."

"It will be very different from going to our city's market," added Mary.

"If we work hard, we will soon **thrive**," remarked Mother. "We will find ways to prosper, and maybe we will be able to sell our eggs in town."

"And our fruits and vegetables," added Mary.

"Will our new house look like our city house?" asked a curious Stewart.

Father patted Stewart and replied, "No, son. It will be small and simple to start. It won't have three stories like our brownstone. It will be one story and made of timber."

As Mary fell asleep that night under the stars, she dreamed of her new home and her new life.

Name: _____ Date: _____

Use "Westward Ho!" to answer Numbers 1 through 7.

1 What evidence from the passage describes the difference between the countryside and the city?

Ⓐ It is not noisy like the city, and we have not seen one building in miles.

Ⓑ I think I shall like living in the country, after all.

Ⓒ As Mary fell asleep that night under the stars, she dreamed of her new home and her new life.

2 Which word from the passage has about the same meaning as *perspective*?

Ⓐ view

Ⓑ wilderness

Ⓒ country

3 How is food on the journey different from food in the city?

Ⓐ There are desserts on the journey.

Ⓑ There are dried foods on the journey.

Ⓒ There are fresh vegetables on the journey.

4 How will the Bond family's land in Oregon compare to the land they had in New York?

Ⓐ It will be much larger.

Ⓑ It will be smaller, but near a river.

Ⓒ It will be about the same size, but prettier.

GO ON →

5 Read this sentence from the passage.

> Father added, "It will be good to rely and
> depend upon our land to grow our food."

Which clue word in the sentence helps to explain what
rely means?

Ⓐ good

Ⓑ depend

Ⓒ grow

6 Read this paragraph from the passage.

> "If we work hard, we will soon thrive," remarked
> Mother. "We will find ways to succeed. Maybe we will
> be able to sell our eggs in town."

Which word from the paragraph has about the same meaning
as *thrive*?

Ⓐ work

Ⓑ succeed

Ⓒ sell

7 How will the Bond's country house be different from their
city house?

Ⓐ It will be larger and made of brownstone.

Ⓑ It will be taller and have three stories.

Ⓒ It will be smaller and made of timber.

GO ON →

Read "Love Canal: A Toxic Community" before you answer
Numbers 8 through 15.

Love Canal: A Toxic Community

A major environmental disaster was in the making during the 1940s. During that time, a chemical company in Niagara Falls, New York began dumping toxic waste in a canal near the river. It is hard to know exactly how many dangerous chemicals filled the dumpsite, but it was **approximately** 21,800 tons.

In 1953, the site was covered up. The city bought it for one dollar! Workers tried to stop the chemicals from seeping out. To seal the landfill, they placed a thick layer of earth over the site.

Creating a Community

Soon after, the land was developed. First, a sewer line was dug. The developers did not know that the layer of earth over the site had been damaged during the digging.

About 100 homes were built. Public schools were built, too. The community was named Love Canal. Soon, people began to notice an odor in the **atmosphere**. There was a choking smell in the air. Waste came up in people's backyards. Chemicals that had been buried for years began seeping into the basements of homes. People got very sick. The country was angered. How could something like this happen?

An Environmental Disaster

Families of Love Canal were eventually forced to leave. The government paid to clean up the toxic land, but it was all too late. People's lives and the environment had already been harmed. The question people asked themselves after this tragedy was: *What can be done to prevent another Love Canal disaster someplace else?*

GO ON →

What Can Be Done?

It is important that measures are taken to prevent environmental disasters. Chemical waste sites must be environmentally safe. Companies must follow strict safety codes. These sites also have to be managed correctly. The government requires these measures to make sure similar tragedies never happen again. And citizens must do what they can to learn about environmental issues. This will help keep our communities safe for generations to come.

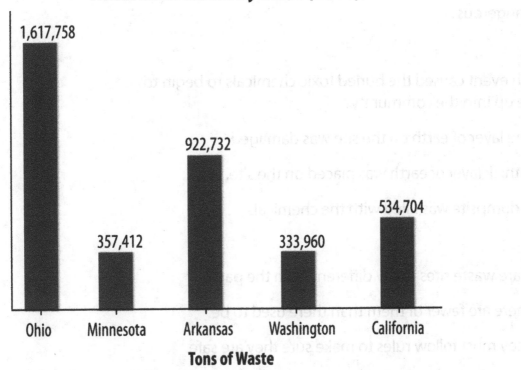

Hazardous Waste By State (2011)

- Ohio: 1,617,758
- Minnesota: 357,412
- Arkansas: 922,732
- Washington: 333,960
- California: 534,704

Tons of Waste

GO ON →

Use "Love Canal: A Toxic Community" to answer Numbers 8 through 15.

8 Read this sentence from the article.

> **It is hard to know exactly how many dangerous chemicals filled the dumpsite, but it was approximately 21,800 tons.**

Which word from the sentence means the OPPOSITE of *approximately*?

Ⓐ hard

Ⓑ exactly

Ⓒ dangerous

9 Which event caused the buried toxic chemicals to begin to come up into the community?

Ⓐ The layer of earth on the site was damaged.

Ⓑ A thick layer of earth was placed on the site.

Ⓒ A dumpsite was filled with the chemicals.

10 How are waste sites today different from the past?

Ⓐ There are fewer of them than there used to be.

Ⓑ They must follow rules to make sure they are safe.

Ⓒ They cause more problems for the environment now.

GO ON →

11 Read these sentences from the article.

> **Soon, people began to notice an odor in the atmosphere. There was a choking smell in the air.**

Which word from the sentences has about the same meaning as *atmosphere*?

Ⓐ odor

Ⓑ smell

Ⓒ air

12 How does the author support the idea that Love Canal was a mistake to build?

Ⓐ by explaining what a dumpsite is

Ⓑ by telling how waste can be harmful

Ⓒ by describing how land is developed

13 What does the government now do as a result of the Love Canal situation?

Ⓐ It tells communities about environmental issues.

Ⓑ It no longer allows companies to dump chemicals.

Ⓒ It makes sure that dumpsites are managed correctly.

GO ON →

14 With which statement would the author most likely agree?

Ⓐ Everyone must all do their part to prevent environmental disasters.

Ⓑ Environmental tragedies like the one at Love Canal cannot always be stopped.

Ⓒ The government needs to do more to stop companies from dumping any type of waste.

15 According to the graph, which two states produced the most hazardous waste in 2011?

Ⓐ Ohio and Arkansas

Ⓑ Ohio and Minnesota

Ⓒ Washington and Minnesota

STOP

Read "Dear Benjie" before you answer Numbers 1 through 7.

Dear Benjie

Benjie knocked on the principal's door.

"Come on in," said Ms. Choy. "How are you, Benjie?"

"I'm fine." Benjie took a deep breath. "I have an idea for the school newspaper. I've noticed some kids are having trouble getting along, so I thought we could put a box outside your office. Students could write letters about problems they're having. They could leave names off the letters."

Ms. Choy smiled. "I like the idea, but what would you do with the letters?"

"I could write a column. I would give **survival** advice and help kids figure out how to get through elementary school!"

Ms. Choy laughed. "You have quite the sense of humor, Benjie. I think your idea is brilliant and very helpful! Your column will have a positive **influence** and effect on our students. What will you call it?"

Benjie laughed. "How about 'Dear Benjie?'"

Benjie's column became wildly popular! The box by Ms. Choy's office was stuffed with letters every Friday, and Benjie always looked forward to writing his responses.

Dear Benjie,

Friend A gets jealous when I play with Friend B. Friend B gets jealous when I play with Friend A. What can I do?

From,
Caught in the Middle

GO ON →

Dear Caught in the Middle,

Why don't you invite both friends over to your house at the same time? Then you can all have fun together!

Sincerely,
Benjie

Everything was going well until one day, Benjie's best friend, Hugo, started ignoring him. Benjie tried talking to him, but Hugo just walked away. Benjie had no one to **intervene**. There wasn't another "Benjie" to help settle his problem. So, he asked his readers for advice!

Dear Students,

A good friend of mine won't talk to me. I've tried asking him what's wrong, but he just ignores me. What can I do?

Sincerely,
Benjie

It was no surprise when many kids offered good advice. Benjie realized that sometimes it's easier helping others solve their problems than solving your own!

A few days went by before Hugo came up to Benjie.

"I'm glad you're ready to talk. I've missed hanging out with you," Benjie said.

"But that's the point, Benjie!" said Hugo. "You've been so busy with your column that you haven't had time to hang out."

Benjie's eyes widened. "You're right! I'm sorry. Why don't you help me write the column on Saturday mornings? Then we can have the rest of the day to hang out."

"Cool idea!" said Hugo. "I can't wait to get started."

GO ON →

Name: _____ Date: _____

Use "Dear Benjie" to answer Numbers 1 through 7.

1 Which words from the passage help to explain the meaning of *survival*?

    Ⓐ having trouble getting along

    Ⓑ how to get through

    Ⓒ became wildly popular

2 Which sentence from the passage best shows how Benjie feels about his new column?

    Ⓐ The box by Ms. Choy's office was stuffed with letters every Friday, and Benjie always looked forward to writing his responses.

    Ⓑ Everything was going well until one day, Benjie's best friend, Hugo, started ignoring him.

    Ⓒ There wasn't another "Benjie" to help settle his problem.

3 What message about helping others does the passage send?

    Ⓐ You can help others by giving advice.

    Ⓑ Writing is the best way to try to help someone.

    Ⓒ If you help someone, that person should help you.

4 Which word from the passage has about the same meaning as *influence*?

    Ⓐ column

    Ⓑ effect

    Ⓒ students

GO ON →

5 Read this sentence from the passage.

> **Benjie had no one to intervene.**

Which word from the passage has about the same meaning as *intervene*?

Ⓐ ignored

Ⓑ settle

Ⓒ asked

6 What does Benjie think about how his friend Hugo feels?

Ⓐ He thinks Hugo does not understand him.

Ⓑ He thinks Hugo is jealous of him.

Ⓒ He thinks Hugo is correct.

7 Which sentence best states the theme of the passage?

Ⓐ Sometimes your own advice is the best advice.

Ⓑ People should try to solve one problem at a time.

Ⓒ A good sense of humor is needed to fix a problem.

GO ON →

Read "PeaceJam" before you answer Numbers 8 through 15.

PeaceJam

What happens when young people and Nobel Peace Prize winners get together? Positive change is what happens!

An Idea Forms

In 1993, a man named Ivan Suvanjieff met a group of troubled kids in Denver. He stopped to talk to them. He asked if they knew about the work of Nobel Peace Prize winner, Desmond Tutu. The kids had heard of him. Tutu uses nonviolent methods to make positive world changes.

Ivan told his friend, Dawn Engle, about his encounter. He thought that if these kids can be enthusiastic about creating change, then other kids could, too.

Dawn worked for a group called Colorado Friends of Tibet. She was able to get a meeting with the Dalai Lama. The Dalai Lama is a well-known religious leader who promotes peace. Dawn and Ivan shared their idea for a program. He liked it. He **enlisted** other Nobel Peace Prize winners like himself to join in to support the cause. Together, they started PeaceJam.

Since then, more than 600,000 young people have been involved in the program. They address world problems including poverty, violence, and human rights.

Studying the Problem

First, the youth leaders in PeaceJam study the problems. They use critical thinking skills. They also research each problem to find its cause.

GO ON →

Getting Inspired

After educating themselves about the problem, they learn about the lives of Nobel Peace Prize winners. They find out how these leaders helped to solve their own countries' problems using nonviolent methods. What is the effect of learning about these leaders? The kids are inspired to take action! They find ways to use their talents and passions to make positive changes.

Call to Action

Through the process, youth leaders become peacebuilders. They try to **restore**, or bring back, peace in troubled areas of the world. They create projects. These projects focus on difficult issues like disease and the environment. The kids register their projects. Then they work to complete them with the help of schools, community centers, and clubs.

Official PeaceJam Groups Around the Globe

KEY
● PeaceJam Locations

North America

Europe

Asia

Africa

South America

Australia

GO ON →

Name: _____ Date: _____

Use "PeaceJam" to answer Numbers 8 through 15.

8 According to the article, what happens when young people and Nobel Peace Prize winners get together?

Ⓐ new friends

Ⓑ positive change

Ⓒ long discussions

9 What caused Ivan and Dawn to create the PeaceJam program?

Ⓐ They met troubled kids who were enthusiastic to create change.

Ⓑ They always wanted to start an organization to promote peace.

Ⓒ They had a meeting with the Dalai Lama, a Nobel Peace Prize winner.

10 Read these sentences from the article.

> He enlisted other Nobel Peace Prize winners like himself to join in to support the cause. Together, they started PeaceJam.

Which phrase from these sentences helps to explain the meaning of *enlisted*?

Ⓐ like himself

Ⓑ to join in

Ⓒ they started

11 Which is NOT an example of the problems that PeaceJam leaders try to solve?

Ⓐ poverty

Ⓑ education

Ⓒ human rights

12 How do the PeaceJam youth leaders start to try to solve a problem?

Ⓐ They get inspired by learning how Nobel Peace Prize winners have solved problems.

Ⓑ They register their projects with organizations that will help them.

Ⓒ They use critical thinking skills to study the problem.

13 Read this sentence from the article.

They try to restore, or bring back, peace in troubled areas of the world.

Which clue words in the sentence help to explain what *restore* means?

Ⓐ try to

Ⓑ bring back

Ⓒ troubled areas

14 What goal do the peacebuilders have when they go through the PeaceJam process?

Ⓐ to end war around the world

Ⓑ to build new organizations

Ⓒ to get a Nobel Peace Prize

15 According to the map, which continent has the most official PeaceJam locations?

Ⓐ Africa

Ⓑ North America

Ⓒ South America

STOP

Exit
Assessment

Read "The *Almost* Perfect Celebration!" before you answer Numbers 1 through 7.

The *Almost* Perfect Celebration!

The kids could hardly wait for their friend Tomas to arrive home on Friday. He had spent the past year living in Brazil where his mom worked at the American Embassy. The kids were planning a surprise party for Saturday afternoon to welcome him home.

"I'll call everyone and ask them to bring snacks," suggested Lamar.

"We can have the party in my backyard. Tomas has always loved marbles, so let's collect some money to buy a marble run. We can set it up on the picnic table," said Lee.

"My older brother can help me bake a cake," suggested Cammie. "The **options** are a choice of strawberry cake, carrot cake, or cinnamon cake."

"Strawberry cake!" yelled Lamar and Lee as they high-fived each other.

On Friday afternoon, Lee took the marble run pieces out of the box. He laid them on the table and then opened the directions. "Whew!" he said to himself. "This is going to take a while to put together."

Soon, Lee began to **encounter**, or come across, a problem. One piece of the marble run was missing. Being creative, he figured out an even better way to put the toy together. Hours later, he was done, and the marble run covered the entire table!

GO ON →

On Saturday morning, Cammie and her brother baked the cake. She was decorating the cake when the phone rang.

"Tell me you didn't bake the cake yet," said Lamar anxiously.

"I'm just about done. Why?"

Lamar took a deep breath. "James told me that Tomas is allergic to wheat."

"Oh, no!" cried Cammie, who had used wheat flour in the cake. "We don't have time to bake a new one, but I think the bakery may have wheat-free cupcakes."

Cammie hung up, and then the phone rang again.

"It's Lee. It's starting to rain!"

"What are we going to do?" Cammie moaned.

"We'll have to move the party inside."

Lee's solution made sense, and Cammie understood his **reasoning**. But it would be hot and crowded in the den.

"It will be difficult, but we'll make it work!" she said. "We'll have to lift the table together and take apart the marble run, but we can put it back together inside."

The kids scrambled, but they did it. At 3:00 P.M., Tomas walked in as everyone yelled, "Surprise!"

"This is the perfect celebration! Thanks, everyone," grinned Tomas.

"Well, it's the *almost* perfect celebration," giggled Cammie. "Wait until you hear what happened!"

GO ON →

Name: _____ Date: _____

Use "The *Almost* Perfect Celebration!" to answer Numbers 1 through 7.

1 Read this paragraph from the passage.

> "My older brother can help me bake a cake," suggested Cammie. "The options are a choice of strawberry cake, carrot cake, or cinnamon cake."

Which words from the paragraph help to explain what *options* means?

Ⓐ older brother

Ⓑ help me bake

Ⓒ a choice of

2 What problem does Lee have as he puts the marble run together?

Ⓐ The toy is missing an important piece.

Ⓑ The toy takes up more space than he thought.

Ⓒ The toy's directions are too hard to understand.

3 Which words from the text give a clue about the meaning of *encounter*?

Ⓐ take a while

Ⓑ come across

Ⓒ an even better way

GO ON →

4 Which event happens first in the passage?

Ⓐ Lamar tells Cammie that Tomas is allergic to wheat.

Ⓑ The kids decide to bake a strawberry cake for Tomas.

Ⓒ Cammie realizes she does not have time to bake a new cake.

5 What evidence from the text gives you a clue about how Cammie will solve the problem with the cake?

Ⓐ She learns that Tomas is allergic to cake flour.

Ⓑ She bakes a cake with her older brother's help.

Ⓒ She thinks the bakery has wheat-free cupcakes.

6 Which words in the passage help you figure out the meaning of the word *reasoning*?

Ⓐ Lee's solution made sense

Ⓑ hot and crowded in the den

Ⓒ we'll make it work

7 What is the last problem the kids have in the passage?

Ⓐ They have to raise money for a toy.

Ⓑ They have to move the party inside.

Ⓒ They have to make food for the party.

GO ON →

Read "A Great Observer" before you answer Numbers 8 through 15.

A Great Observer

Jane Goodall was born in London, England, on April 3, 1934. As a young girl, she was **passionate** about animals. Jane showed strong feelings for a stuffed animal her father gave her. She carried her toy chimpanzee, Jubilee, everywhere she went. She also dreamed of living in Africa after reading a children's book. The book was called *The Story of Dr. Dolittle*. The story is about a doctor who can talk to animals. He travels to Africa.

Heading to Africa

Jane's dream finally came true when she was 23 years old. She saved her money and traveled to Africa to visit a friend. Jane met a well-known scientist there. His name was Dr. Louis Leakey. He saw that Jane had a passion for wild animals. So, Leakey hired her as an assistant. Jane's job was to study chimpanzees and their behavior.

Observing Chimpanzees

Jane was dedicated to her job. She had to work very hard to gain the chimpanzees' trust. As a result, the animals finally allowed her near them. Soon, she made an important **breakthrough**, or discovery, in her research. She learned that a pair of chimpanzees could make tools. They stripped the leaves off twigs and used the twigs to find termites in the ground. This showed her that chimpanzees were very smart. She named the chimpanzees David Greybeard and Goliath. Jane also watched chimpanzees eating small animals. Until then, many people thought chimpanzees only ate plants.

GO ON →

Making the World a Better Place

Jane has written many articles and books about nature. She tries to get young people to help make the world a better place. In 1977, she created the Jane Goodall Institute. It helps to save forests and animal habitats. Jane inspires people everywhere. She still has her favorite stuffed animal, Jubilee, to this day. Jane once said:

Quite apart from Jubilee, I have been fascinated by live animals from the time when I first learned to crawl. One of my earliest recollections is of the day that I hid in a small stuffy henhouse in order to see how a hen laid an egg. I emerged after about five hours. The whole household had apparently been searching for me...

– Jane Goodall

GO ON →

Use "A Great Observer" to answer Numbers 8 through 15.

8 Read this sentence from the article.

> **As a young girl, she was passionate about animals.**

Which text evidence gives clues about the meaning of *passionate*?

(A) Jane showed strong feelings for a stuffed animal her father gave her.

(B) She carried her toy chimpanzee, Jubilee, everywhere she went.

(C) The story is about a doctor who can talk to animals.

9 What caused Jane to dream about visiting Africa one day?

(A) She had a friend who lived in Africa.

(B) She learned about Africa from her father.

(C) She read a book about a doctor who travels to Africa.

10 Why did Dr. Louis Leakey hire Jane for a job?

(A) He saw her passion for wild animals.

(B) He heard that she was a good assistant.

(C) He knew that she worked with chimpanzees.

GO ON →

11 Which detail from the text supports the author's point of view that Jane was dedicated to her job?

Ⓐ Jane's dream finally came true when she was 23 years old.

Ⓑ Jane's job was to study chimpanzees and their behavior.

Ⓒ She had to work very hard to gain the chimpanzees' trust.

12 Read this sentence from the article.

> **Soon, she made an important breakthrough, or discovery, in her research.**

Which clue word helps explain what *breakthrough* means?

Ⓐ important

Ⓑ discovery

Ⓒ research

13 Which sentence in the article signals a cause-and-effect relationship?

Ⓐ As a result, the animals finally allowed her near them.

Ⓑ She named the chimpanzees David Greybeard and Goliath.

Ⓒ Jane also watched chimpanzees eating small animals.

14 What does the author think of Jane at the end of the article?

Ⓐ She knows more about chimpanzees than anyone else.

Ⓑ She should write more books about nature.

Ⓒ She is a good role model for others.

15 Based on the quote at the end of the article, why did Jane hide in a henhouse?

Ⓐ She wanted to see how a hen laid an egg.

Ⓑ She wanted to see a hen for the first time.

Ⓒ She wanted to see if a hen would play with her.

STOP

Read "A Natural Wonder" before you answer Numbers 1 though 8.

A Natural Wonder

More than Stars

Since long ago, people have been fascinated with the night sky. Besides the stars and Moon, a beautiful display of colored lights can sometimes be seen above us. In the northern half of Earth, it is called the aurora borealis. It is also known as the northern lights.

These lights are most noticeable in Alaska, Canada, and the Arctic. They can be white, green, pink, red, and blue. Many colors can be **detected** without a telescope, but the reddish colors are the hardest to see.

What Causes the Northern Lights?

In 1896, a Norwegian astronomer named Kristian Birkeland had a **theory**. His idea was based on his discoveries as well as conclusions he made. He believed that sunspots caused the northern lights. These are patches of cool areas on the surface of the Sun.

Since then, astronomers came up with a different idea. They believe that solar wind is the source for these lights. Particles with electric charges flow from the Sun. The particles are trapped in the wind and pulled into the atmosphere by Earth's magnetic force. These particles are made up of different colors. You might even see wide stripes, or bands, of light. They look like they are dancing across the sky!

GO ON →

Viewing the Northern Lights

For astronomers to see the northern lights, the weather conditions have to be just right. There must be a clear, dark sky.

Astronomers set up powerful telescopes to watch the light display. However, sometimes cloudy or hazy conditions make the lights difficult to see. To see the northern lights more clearly, telescopes are attached to satellites. Then, the satellites are sent into outer space. These telescopes are called satellite telescopes. They send very clear pictures back to Earth. Astronomers can then study the pictures to make a better **observation**. What they see helps them figure out why the northern lights color our sky.

The Northern Lights

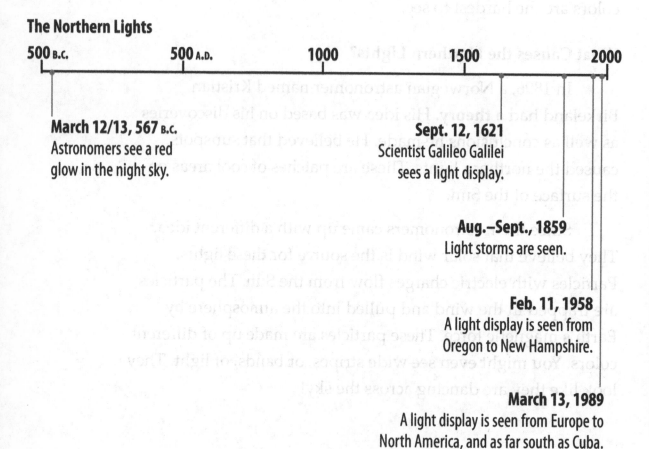

500 B.C.   500 A.D.   1000   1500   2000

March 12/13, 567 B.C.
Astronomers see a red glow in the night sky.

Sept. 12, 1621
Scientist Galileo Galilei sees a light display.

Aug.–Sept., 1859
Light storms are seen.

Feb. 11, 1958
A light display is seen from Oregon to New Hampshire.

March 13, 1989
A light display is seen from Europe to North America, and as far south as Cuba.

GO ON →

Use "A Natural Wonder" to answer Numbers 1 through 8.

1 Read this sentence from the article.

> **Many colors can be detected without a telescope,
> but the reddish colors are the hardest to see.**

Which clue word from the sentence helps to explain what *detected* means?

Ⓐ colors

Ⓑ reddish

Ⓒ see

2 What happens after solar wind particles get trapped in the wind?

Ⓐ They are pulled into Earth's atmosphere.

Ⓑ They flow away from the Sun.

Ⓒ They form sunspots.

3 Which word from the article has about the same meaning as *theory*?

Ⓐ astronomer

Ⓑ idea

Ⓒ patches

4 Which details from the text describe a problem for astronomers hoping to see the northern lights?

Ⓐ stripes, or bands, of light

Ⓑ a clear, dark sky

Ⓒ cloudy or hazy conditions

5 Read these sentences from the article.

> Then, the satellites are sent into outer space. These telescopes are called satellite telescopes. They send very clear pictures back to Earth. Astronomers can then study the pictures to make a better observation.

Which phrase from the sentences helps you understand the meaning of *observation*?

Ⓐ sent into outer space

Ⓑ send very clear pictures

Ⓒ study the pictures

6 Which event must happen first for scientists to see the northern lights?

Ⓐ Weather conditions must be just right.

Ⓑ People must send satellites into outer space.

Ⓒ Astronomers must figure out what the northern lights are.

GO ON →

7 What is the solution when the northern lights cannot be seen due to the weather?

Ⓐ People travel into outer space to watch them.

Ⓑ Satellite telescopes send images back to Earth.

Ⓒ Astronomers travel to different places on Earth.

8 According to the time line, in what year were light storms seen?

Ⓐ 1621

Ⓑ 1859

Ⓒ 1989

Read "The Princess and the Pea" before you answer Numbers 9 through 15.

The Princess and the Pea

Once upon a time, there was a prince in search of a princess. He went from village to village looking for the perfect princess to marry. His father and mother, the king and queen, said it was his **destiny**. So, the prince knew it must be his fate to marry a beautiful, loving, and generous princess.

However, the more he searched, the more the prince became sad and frustrated. He could not find a young woman with all of the traits a princess should have, so the prince continued his search around the world. Each time he met a new princess, he always found something wrong. One was beautiful, but not loving. Another was generous, but could be mean. Each time he left a castle, he wondered, "Will I ever meet the perfect princess?" Finally, the prince returned home.

One evening, there was a terrible storm with loud roars of thunder followed by bright flashes of lightning. Rain pounded against the castle rooftops. It was quite a frightful night.

Suddenly, there was a knock at the castle door. "Who would be calling on us this evening?" wondered the king as he went to answer the door.

Standing there was a young woman, soaking wet from the rain. Streams of water ran down her hair and face and into her shoes. Although she was wet, the prince still found her to be very beautiful. Kindly, she asked, "Please, may I enter the castle? I am a princess and I have lost my way."

GO ON →

As the king led the princess inside, the queen thought to herself, "Hmmm. We shall see if she is a true princess." Then the queen went to a bedroom and removed the bedding and even the mattress. She placed a single pea on the bed frame. Afterward, she placed twenty mattresses and many layers of soft bedding on top of the tiny pea.

The queen invited the princess to sleep on top of the mattresses. She soon fell fast asleep.

In the morning, the family gathered for breakfast.

"How did you sleep?" asked the ever-hopeful prince.

"I am sorry to say that I slept poorly," sighed the princess. "I tossed and turned all night, and my whole body is black and blue. I think that I was lying on something hard in my bed, but I could not find any way to improve my **situation**!"

The family sighed with relief, for only a real princess could feel a tiny pea through twenty layers of mattresses. This is because princesses have very delicate skin.

The prince was joyful and asked the princess to be his wife. They were married that very month and lived happily ever after.

GO ON →

Use "The Princess and the Pea" to answer Numbers 9 through 15.

9 Read this sentence from the passage.

> His father and mother, the king and queen, said it was
> his destiny.

Which word from the passage has about the same meaning
as *destiny*?

(A) fate

(B) princess

(C) world

10 Why does the prince have trouble finding a princess to marry?

(A) No one has all of the correct traits.

(B) None of the princesses are beautiful.

(C) All of the princesses are married already.

11 Compared to when the prince leaves his castle, when he returns
he is more _____.

(A) confused

(B) hopeful

(C) upset

GO ON →

12 What does the queen want to know about the young woman who comes to the castle?

Ⓐ if she is who she claims to be

Ⓑ if she will continue to be kind

Ⓒ if she can get along with her son

13 Which words from the text help to explain the meaning of *situation*?

Ⓐ lying on something hard

Ⓑ could not find

Ⓒ sighed with relief

14 How does the royal family know that the young woman is a princess?

Ⓐ A princess is always honest to whomever she meets.

Ⓑ A princess is still beautiful even when she is soaking wet.

Ⓒ A princess is delicate and would feel a pea under a mattress.

15 How does the prince feel differently by the end of the passage?

Ⓐ He feels badly because the princess slept so poorly.

Ⓑ He feels pleased to have found a true princess to marry.

Ⓒ He feels tired from having to search so long for a princess.

STOP

Read "A Movie Adventure" before you answer Numbers 1 through 7.

A Movie Adventure

Davy, Hugo, and Lea paid for their tickets to see the new *Desert Martians* movie. The friends were especially excited because they had been learning about desert environments in their outdoor adventure class.

Davy tapped his backpack and said, "I've got snacks for our hike later."

"And I have water to last for several days," added Hugo.

They entered the darkened theater and found that it was completely empty!

Lea pointed toward the front of the theater. "Everything will look huge with our 3-D glasses on!"

Toward the end of the movie, Hugo sighed as the Martians were about to leave the desert. "This movie is really boring. Nothing exciting is happening!"

Just then, a Martian pointed toward the kids, and suddenly, a magnetic force sucked them right through the movie screen where they landed in a pile of sand.

"Run toward the rocks!" shouted Davy.

As they ran, they heard a robotic voice say, "It is time to go, so leave them." Then, a spaceship rose up into the sky and disappeared.

Just then, an animal cried out in the distance, *"Owooooooh!"*

"What's that?" asked Hugo as he looked around.

GO ON →

"It's just a coyote," replied Davy confidently. "It sounds like it is far away, but we should come up with a plan to get home before dark."

"Let's do the **S.T.O.P.** plan," Hugo suggested.

Stop! Take a deep breath.

Think! Don't panic.

Observe! Look around you.

Plan! **Devise** a way to get back to our real lives."

"Great idea!" grinned Lea. "Thankfully we have granola bars and bottled water to get us through this."

"And we can get additional nutrition if we need it from the cactus fruit that grows here," Davy added.

Hugo had another good suggestion. "Right before we got sucked into the movie, I noticed a seam in the screen. Let's go back to where we entered and try to find our way out."

The kids started heading back from where they came when they noticed a flat area in the distance. Davy reached out as they approached it and found that it was the screen! He moved his fingers over it and, sure enough, he felt the seam.

Davy pulled a spike off a nearby cactus and sliced through the seam of the movie screen. Then he gently opened it and stepped through. The kids were back in the theater again!

Hugo got out some glue from his backpack and closed the seam. "We should **congratulate** ourselves," he said with a smile. "I'm really proud that we got out of the desert safely!"

Lea chuckled and shook her head. "No one is going to believe this story!"

GO ON →

Use "A Movie Adventure" to answer Numbers 1 through 7.

1 What evidence from the text shows how Hugo is resourceful?

Ⓐ He carries a backpack to the movie.

Ⓑ He remembers to bring snacks for the hike.

Ⓒ He has enough water to last for several days.

2 What evidence from the passage shows how the kids are prepared for an outdoor hike?

Ⓐ They go to the movies.

Ⓑ They have food and water.

Ⓒ They bring their 3-D glasses.

3 Why is Hugo's S.T.O.P. plan a good idea?

Ⓐ It will keep them away from the coyote.

Ⓑ It will help them stay calm and aware.

Ⓒ It will allow them to rest for a while.

4 Read these sentences from the passage.

> *"Plan!* Devise a way to get back to our real lives."

Which clue word from the sentences helps to explain what *devise* means?

Ⓐ plan

Ⓑ get

Ⓒ real

GO ON →

5 How is Davy's knowledge about nature useful?

Ⓐ He knows that coyotes are dangerous.

Ⓑ He knows that they need to get home.

Ⓒ He knows that cactus fruit is nutritious.

6 What evidence from the text shows an example of being resourceful?

Ⓐ going back to the movie theater again

Ⓑ running toward a flat area in the distance

Ⓒ using a cactus spike to open up the movie seam

7 Read this sentence from the passage.

"We should congratulate ourselves," he said with a smile.

Which sentence from the text gives a clue about the meaning of *congratulate*?

Ⓐ The kids were back in the theater again!

Ⓑ "I'm really proud that we got out of the desert safely!"

Ⓒ "No one is going to believe this story!"

Read "The Long Journey" before you answer Numbers 8 through 15.

The Long Journey

Birds are amazing creatures! It is hard not to look at them in awe. Have you ever looked up in the sky and seen a **formation** of birds flying in the shape of a *V*? The flock of geese or cranes form a perfect arrangement. They are all flying in the same direction. The flock seems to have a purpose and sense of where it is going. The birds you see may be migrating, which means they are traveling from one habitat, or home, to another.

Why Migrate?

Many animals migrate. They do it in different ways. They may travel by land, air, or water. Some walk great distances, while others fly across entire continents. Some animals even swim through wide oceans!

There are many reasons why animals migrate. Each autumn, many birds fly thousands of miles south. They are seeking warmer weather. Monarch butterflies in North America also migrate. Some travel nearly 3,000 miles. They begin in southern Canada and end in central Mexico. Like birds, they are in search of mild weather. It is incredible to think how such a small creature can travel so far!

Elephant seals migrate, too. They go where they can breed and give birth to their pups, or seal babies.

Hoofed animals migrate in search of plants and grasses during the colder months. For example, herds of elk, deer, and antelope look for green grass. Their search for new food sources begins when the snow arrives.

GO ON →

Exit Assessment · Unit 3

A Difficult Journey

The long journey during migration can be tough on animals. Some may have **obstacles** along the way. These problems get in the way of the animals' movement and progress. For example, some animals may have to escape predators. Others may face barriers built by humans, such as power lines, tall buildings, or electrical towers.

Once animals arrive at their destination, their habitat from the previous year may no longer be there. They may have to **reconstruct** it, or build it again, before they can settle there safely for the season.

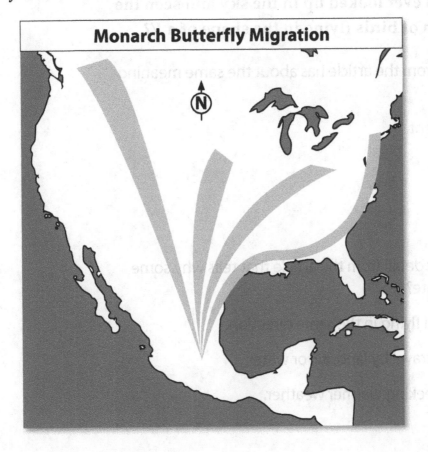

Monarch Butterfly Migration

Use "The Long Journey" to answer Numbers 8 through 15.

8 Which sentence from the article best supports the author's point of view that birds are amazing creatures?

Ⓐ It is hard not to look at them in awe.

Ⓑ Some animals even swim through wide oceans!

Ⓒ Their search for new food sources begins when the snow arrives.

9 Read this sentence from the article.

Have you ever looked up in the sky and seen the formation of birds flying in the shape of a V?

Which word from the article has about the same meaning as *formation*?

Ⓐ arrangement

Ⓑ direction

Ⓒ purpose

10 Which is a key detail from the article that tells why some animals migrate?

Ⓐ They are all flying in the same direction.

Ⓑ They may travel by land, air, or water.

Ⓒ They are seeking warmer weather.

GO ON →

11 Which sentence from the article best supports the author's point of view that monarch butterflies travel far for their size?

Ⓐ There are many reasons why animals migrate.

Ⓑ Some travel nearly 3,000 miles.

Ⓒ Like birds, they are in search of mild weather.

12 Read this sentence from the article.

Some may have obstacles along the way.

Which clues from the article tell the meaning of *obstacles*?

Ⓐ long journey

Ⓑ get in the way

Ⓒ movement and progress

13 What is the main idea of the section "A Difficult Journey"?

Ⓐ Animals may face barriers that have been built by humans.

Ⓑ Animals may have to rebuild habitats at their final destination.

Ⓒ Animals may encounter some problems during their migration.

GO ON →

14 Read this paragraph from the article.

> Once animals arrive at their destination, their habitat from the previous year may no longer be there. They may have to reconstruct it, or build it again, before they can settle there safely for the season.

Which words from the paragraph have about the same meaning as *reconstruct*?

Ⓐ no longer be there

Ⓑ build it again

Ⓒ settle there safely

15 How many monarch butterfly migration routes are shown in the diagram?

Ⓐ 4

Ⓑ 3

Ⓒ 1

STOP

Read "Pecos Bill Rides a Tornado" before you answer Numbers 1 through 7.

Pecos Bill Rides a Tornado

Here's a story about the best bronco rider east and west of the great Mississippi River. His name was Pecos Bill. He was so good that not even the wildest horse could throw him. One time, Bill just happened to be traveling through Kansas when he decided to ride something very unusual. He did it just for the fun of it!

In the distance, Bill saw the sky turning green and black. At first, the cowboy thought there was a good storm starting to form. So he kept riding across the plain. But Bill started hearing a great roar of noise. He turned back to look a second time.

Coming at him at a fast pace was a giant funnel-shaped cloud! It reached from the sky to the ground. The cyclone was moving so fast that Bill was sure the noise would wake up all of the farmers from here to China at the same time! Bill's eyes popped open in surprise. Dust and dirt began to **circulate** in a giant dark mass of wind. It was whirling around and around, making Bill's head spin.

When the moment was just right, Bill lassoed that tornado. He shoved it to the ground. In one mighty jump, Bill was on the back of that whirling cyclone, riding it just like a bronco!

As it moved south toward Texas, it tied those windy rivers into knots. It sped through forests so fast that it knocked down trees. It flattened them to the ground. The forest now looked so flat that farmers here renamed the area Stakes Plains.

GO ON →

While the tornado became angrier and angrier, Bill became calmer and calmer. He occasionally had to steer the tornado as they headed west. So he gave that nasty thing a jab with his boot heels.

As they passed Arizona, the tornado started to turn into rain. Bill looked down at the flow of rushing water. And this is no **exaggeration**! Truth be told, when Bill looked down again, he saw the rain cut the biggest, deepest, most colorful canyon in seconds! Now when that river calmed down, folks named that wonderful place the Grand Canyon.

From there, it was a quick ride to California. The tornado had done exhausted itself when Pecos Bill fell off. He smacked down on the sandy desert. He fell so hard that the ground sank deep down. When folks saw this flat, barren place, they called it Death Valley.

Bill's wild and expert tornado riding was also how the rodeo got started. Though these days, most cowboys stick to riding broncos!

Use "Pecos Bill Rides a Tornado" to answer Numbers 1 through 7.

1 Who is the narrator of the passage?

Ⓐ a speaker who is not part of the story

Ⓑ one of the farmers in the story

Ⓒ the character of Pecos Bill

GO ON →

2 Which evidence from the text supports the narrator's point of view that Pecos Bill was the best bronco rider?

(A) He was so good that not even the wildest horse could throw him.

(B) One time, Bill just happened to be traveling through Kansas when he decided to ride something very unusual.

(C) When the moment was just right, Bill lassoed that tornado.

3 Which detail from the text does the narrator exaggerate to show that this passage is a tall tale?

(A) Coming at him at a fast pace was a giant funnel-shaped cloud!

(B) It sped through forests so fast that it knocked down trees.

(C) He occasionally had to steer the tornado as they headed west.

4 Read this sentence from the passage.

Dust and dirt began to circulate in a giant dark mass of wind.

Which sentence from the passage gives a clue about the meaning of *circulate*?

(A) But Bill started hearing a great roar of noise.

(B) Bill's eyes popped open in surprise.

(C) It was whirling around and around, making Bill's head spin!

GO ON →

5 For which event does the passage NOT provide an explanation?

(A) how the rodeo got started

(B) how people came to settle in the West

(C) how the western landscape was formed

6 Read this sentence from the passage.

And this is no exaggeration!

Which words from the passage mean the OPPOSITE of *exaggeration*?

(A) truth be told

(B) calmed down

(C) wonderful place

7 What did Bill discover about the land while passing through Arizona?

(A) The forest was flattened into a plain.

(B) The sandy desert ground sank deep down.

(C) The water cut a big, deep, and colorful canyon.

GO ON →

Read "Maya Angelou" before you answer Numbers 8 through 15.

Maya Angelou

Growing Up in the South

Marguerite Johnson was born in Missouri, on April 4, 1928. When she was three years old, she and her brother moved to Arkansas. They lived with their grandmother in a small town. There, the children faced discrimination because they were African Americans. She would write about these experiences later in life. Through her grandmother and extended family, she learned about African American values and traditions.

Marguerite's brother, Bailey, had a stutter and would call her "My," meaning "My sister." After reading a book about the Maya Indians, Bailey gave her the nickname "Maya." This is the name Dr. Angelou calls herself today.

Performer and Activist

As a teenager, Maya loved the arts and was very talented. She expressed herself through song, dance, and theater. In the mid-1950s, she **commenced**, or started, her professional life. She toured Europe and performed in the opera.

In 1960, she moved to Africa and worked as an editor, writer, and teacher. Maya also had a gift for languages. She learned how to read and speak five additional languages besides English.

When Maya moved back to the United States, she helped Dr. Martin Luther King, Jr. She became involved with the Civil Rights movement. Maya was deeply affected when Dr. King was assassinated on her birthday in 1968.

GO ON →

Writer and Poet

Soon after King's death, Maya began writing a book about her life. The book was published in 1970. It was called *I Know Why the Caged Bird Sings*. The book **astounded** the world, amazing and touching the hearts and minds of people of all ages.

Maya continues to write, and many people today wait in **anticipation** for her poems and essays. They look forward to reading her words. She has written more than 30 books and was awarded the Presidential Medal of Freedom in 2011 for her writing. It is the highest honor a person can receive. No one is more deserving than Maya—an amazing poet, educator, and person.

In Maya's Own Words	
About Work	"Nothing will work unless you do."
About Love	"If you have only one smile in you, give it to the people you love."
About Writing	"The idea is to write it so that people hear it and it slides through the brain and goes straight to the heart."
About Talent	"I believe that every person is born with talent."

Use "Maya Angelou" to answer Numbers 8 through 15.

8 Why does the author include details about Maya's childhood?

Ⓐ to show how Maya was talented even as a child

Ⓑ to show how Maya learned early how to sing, dance, and act

Ⓒ to show how events helped to make Maya the person she is today

9 Read these sentences from the article.

> She expressed herself through song, dance, and theater. In the mid-1950s, she commenced, or started, her professional life. She toured Europe and performed in the opera.

Which word from these sentences has about the same meaning as *commenced*?

Ⓐ expressed

Ⓑ started

Ⓒ toured

10 What evidence from the text best supports the author's point of view that Maya was gifted with words?

Ⓐ As a teenager, Maya loved the arts and was very talented.

Ⓑ She learned how to read and speak five additional languages besides English.

Ⓒ She became involved with the Civil Rights movement.

GO ON →

11 Read this sentence from the article.

> **The book astounded the world, amazing and touching the hearts and minds of people of all ages.**

Which word from the sentence helps to explain what *astounded* means?

(A) amazing

(B) hearts

(C) all

12 What evidence from the article best supports the author's point of view that Maya's writing is important?

(A) When Maya moved back to the United States, she helped Dr. Martin Luther King, Jr.

(B) Soon after King's death, Maya began writing a book about her life.

(C) She has written more than 30 books and was awarded the Presidential Medal of Freedom in 2011 for her writing.

13 Read these sentences from the article.

> **Maya continues to write, and many people today wait in anticipation for her poems and essays.**

Which evidence from the article gives a clue about the meaning of *anticipation*?

(A) look forward to

(B) was awarded

(C) is more deserving

GO ON →

Name: _____ Date: _____

14 With which statement would the author most likely agree?

Ⓐ Maya Angelou uses her talents in helpful ways.

Ⓑ Maya Angelou is the best writer in the United States.

Ⓒ Maya Angelou expresses herself differently from most writers.

15 Which quote in the chart supports the idea that people can be moved by words?

Ⓐ About Love

Ⓑ About Work

Ⓒ About Writing

STOP

Read "A Discussion of Rights" before you answer Numbers 1 through 7.

A Discussion of Rights

It is a cool summer day in 1776. Elizabeth Miller invites her friends for a morning of sewing and companionship. They live in a Massachusetts Colony and are waiting for word about the meeting of the Continental Congress. The women are hoping that the colonies break free from Great Britain.

"What news have you heard from Philadelphia?" said Elizabeth to the group as they were seated around a warm hearth.

"I know the men will be voting for independence, but I wish *we* had the right to vote as well!" exclaimed Martha Carpenter with a frown.

"We must take small steps and be patient, for it is a **gradual** process, my dear," smiled Elizabeth.

Martha chimed in again. "My friend, Abigail Adams, wrote to her husband, John. She asked him to 'remember the ladies' when they make new laws for our country."

"And what was Mr. Adams's response?" asked Mrs. Goodwin.

Martha frowned and replied, "He said: 'I cannot but laugh.'"

"But John is a good man," said Elizabeth. "He values Abigail's opinions even if he cannot **guarantee**, or promise, that women will gain the right to vote."

GO ON →

"I agree," responded Mrs. Goodwin. "Also, this meeting is about our independence from Great Britain. That *must* happen first. However, John Adams has influence. He will make every effort to do what is right."

Martha nodded. "But we cannot drop the voting issue. I fear that if we do, we will never gain this right. As women, we have few rights. All of our possessions are owned by our husbands, except for you Mrs. Goodwin. You now own your husband's home and business since he passed away."

"But we are fortunate, too!" said Elizabeth reassuringly. "Our husbands are good and kind, and we can even cast a vote on their behalf when they are ill."

"I am fearful that once the colonies declare independence, we will not be able to do that." Mrs. Goodwin warmed her hands by the fire. She continued, "The men in power say that 'all men are created equal.' They do not mention women."

Elizabeth responded, "I am optimistic. I believe that the **prospect** for gaining our voting rights is good. There is a chance we will also vote one day."

Martha smiled as she commented, "You are an optimist at heart, Elizabeth! Your positive attitude is just what these women need. I do agree that more women are enjoying freedoms. We have a female teacher and a doctor in our community! This is a change in the right direction."

"I am doubtful, but I do hope that you both are right," sighed Mrs. Goodwin.

GO ON →

Use "A Discussion of Rights" to answer Numbers 1 through 7.

1 Compared to Mrs. Goodwin, Elizabeth is more _____.

Ⓐ confused

Ⓑ hopeful

Ⓒ selfish

2 Which words from the passage have a similar meaning to the word *gradual*?

Ⓐ take small steps

Ⓑ be patient

Ⓒ chimed in

3 Read this paragraph from the passage.

> "But John is a good man," said Elizabeth. "He values Abigail's opinions even if he cannot guarantee, or promise, that women will gain the right to vote."

Which clue word from the paragraph helps to explain what *guarantee* means?

Ⓐ promise

Ⓑ gain

Ⓒ vote

GO ON →

Name:_____ **Date:**_____

4 How is Mrs. Goodwin's situation different from Martha and Elizabeth's situation?

   Ⓐ She is one of the few women who is allowed to vote.

   Ⓑ All of her possessions are owned by her husband's family.

   Ⓒ She owns her husband's home and business because he passed away.

5 How does Mrs. Goodwin act compared to the other women?

   Ⓐ She is angrier at the women's husbands.

   Ⓑ She is more doubtful that there will be change.

   Ⓒ She is more upset about the rights that women do not have.

6 Which word from the passage has about the same meaning as *prospect*?

   Ⓐ power

   Ⓑ rights

   Ⓒ chance

7 Which opinion do all the women share in the passage?

   Ⓐ Women should have the right to vote.

   Ⓑ Women already enjoy many important rights.

   Ⓒ Women have a good chance of gaining voting rights.

GO ON →

Read "Rising Seas" before you answer Numbers 8 through 15.

Rising Seas

Scientists today know that sea levels have been rising steadily. But the ocean is rising at an alarming rate in some areas of the country.

Studies show that miles of the United States' northeastern coastline are at risk. This area of land reaches from North Carolina to New England. Cities on the coast, like New York and Boston, will be hit the hardest by the rising seas. The water is rising at a fast rate there. The rate is three to four times faster than in other parts of the country.

Causes

Why is this happening? Large ice sheets are melting in parts of the northern Atlantic Ocean. Some scientists believe this is a result of climate change. The glacial melt causes a change in the movement of the ocean currents. This makes the sea expand and rise.

Other factors can cause sea levels to rise. The land is moving. It is rising up in some areas. It is sinking down in others. Wind patterns can cause more water to collect in some places. These factors make it difficult for scientists to predict exactly how much sea levels will rise in the future.

Researchers continue to **evaluate** their findings. Through research, they have been able to estimate the rate at which the water is rising. They also try to study the rate at which ice is melting, though this can be hard to know.

GO ON →

Can We Stop It?

Why are rising sea levels a problem? Higher sea levels cause flooding to be much worse in coastal areas during storms and hurricanes.

By the year 2100, the ocean may have risen by more than a foot in some places. We must find a solution quickly. How will scientists **identify** a way to solve the problem? Governments can do studies to find ways to slow down climate change. Cities can inspect their water systems. It is important that the systems are working properly in the event of a flood. Engineers and scientists are looking for ways to help prepare coastal cities for the effects of rising sea levels. This can cost millions of dollars in funding. So, support from the government is necessary to find a solution.

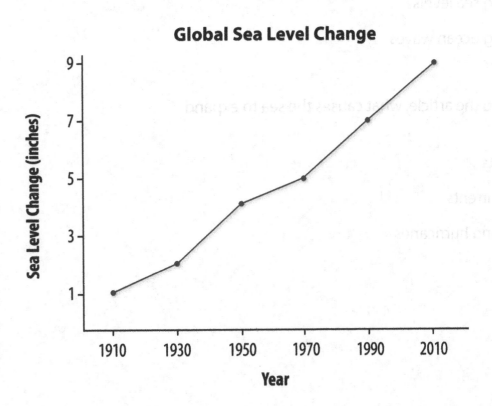

Global Sea Level Change

Use "Rising Seas" to answer Numbers 8 through 15.

8 Which evidence from the article supports the author's point of view that sea levels are rising too quickly in some places?

Ⓐ Scientists today know that sea levels have been rising steadily.

Ⓑ Cities on the coast, like New York and Boston, will be hit the hardest by the rising seas.

Ⓒ The rate is three to four times faster than in other parts of country.

9 What do scientists believe is causing large ice sheets to melt in the Atlantic Ocean?

Ⓐ changing climate

Ⓑ changing sea levels

Ⓒ changing ocean waves

10 According to the article, what causes the sea to expand and rise?

Ⓐ ice sheets

Ⓑ ocean currents

Ⓒ storms and hurricanes

11 Read these sentences from the article.

> **Researchers continue to evaluate their findings.**
> **Through research, they have been able to estimate**
> **the rate at which the water is rising.**

Which word from these sentences has about the same
meaning as *evaluate*?

(A) continue

(B) estimate

(C) rising

12 Compared to low sea levels, high sea levels cause
more _____.

(A) flooding

(B) glaciers

(C) wind

13 Read this sentence from the article.

> **How will scientists identify a way to solve**
> **the problem?**

Which word or phrase from the article has about the same
meaning as *identify*?

(A) find

(B) slow down

(C) inspect

GO ON →

14 Which sentence from the article supports the author's position that governments should help to find a solution to rising seas?

Ⓐ Other factors can cause sea levels to rise.

Ⓑ They also try to study the rate at which ice is melting, though this can be hard to know.

Ⓒ This can cost millions of dollars in funding.

15 Which evidence from the article does the graph support?

Ⓐ The land around us is always moving.

Ⓑ Ocean levels are rising at faster rates.

Ⓒ Cities should inspect their water systems.

STOP

Read "There's No Place Like Home!" before you answer Numbers 1 through 7.

There's No Place Like Home!

Every Saturday, Ana and her older brother, Matt, woke up by 7:00 AM and spent the entire day volunteering at their local animal shelter. They were dropped off by 8:00 AM sharp and stayed until 2:00 PM doing a variety of jobs.

Ana and Matt fed the rescued animals and cleaned their cages. They cradled the cats and played with them. Their favorite job was to walk the dogs through the neighborhood. Matt and Ana could each walk two dogs at a time, with one leash in each hand.

"Whoa, Butch!" said Matt as the little dog tugged on the leash. "Wait while I hook Spotty's leash to his collar."

Matt finished attaching the leash to the bigger dog's collar and soon they were out the door.

"Brrrr," said Ana as she shivered. "It was so warm yesterday, but today it is positively **frigid**!"

The siblings walked briskly through the neighborhood and chatted about what happened during the week at school.

"I joined a civic leadership group," said Ana.

"What do you do?" asked Matt.

"I'm supposed to think of a community project that I can start. Maybe you can help me think of something that is worthwhile."

"I would love to!" said Matt. "How about…"

Suddenly, Butch jerked the leash forward and it snapped **abruptly** as the dog took off running. He rushed into Mrs. Butler's yard and dived into her flowerbed.

"No, Butch!" yelled Matt, running after him.

Mrs. Butler happened to be on her front porch. She laughed in amusement.

"Don't worry!" she said. "I wish I had a dog with such energy and spirit. I could take him into town when I do an **errand**. I would take him to the gardening shop or post office to keep me company."

Ana and Matt turned and looked at each other. "Mrs. Butler, why don't you adopt Butch? Besides being energetic, he's really a sweet and loving dog," said Ana excitedly.

"Why, that's a great idea! I'll walk back to the shelter with you and look into it." Mrs. Butler got her purse, and then the group headed back to the shelter.

That afternoon after work, Matt snapped his fingers. "I've got an idea for your civic leadership project!"

"What is it? Tell me!" exclaimed Ana.

"Why don't you help find homes for the animals at the shelter by pairing them up with people in the community? I could help you!" Matt grinned.

"That is a fantastic idea! What could be better? Helping animals is a cause that is very dear to me." Ana clapped her hands together. "We can set up a small, not-for-profit group and call it 'There's No Place Like Home!'"

Use "There's No Place Like Home!" to answer Numbers 1 through 7.

1 Who is narrating this passage?

Ⓐ Ana

Ⓑ Mrs. Butler

Ⓒ a speaker not in the story

2 What do Ana and Matt think about volunteering at the animal shelter?

Ⓐ They try to get away by visiting Mrs. Butler.

Ⓑ They enjoy helping out and walking the dogs.

Ⓒ They would rather join a few more school activities.

3 Read this paragraph from the passage.

> "Brrrr," said Ana as she shivered. "It was so warm yesterday, but today it is positively frigid!"

Which word from the paragraph means the OPPOSITE of *frigid*?

Ⓐ shivered

Ⓑ warm

Ⓒ positively

4 Why does Ana join a civic leadership group?

Ⓐ to have something to do on Saturdays

Ⓑ to volunteer at the animal shelter

Ⓒ to help out the community

GO ON →

5 Read this paragraph from the passage.

> Suddenly, Butch jerked the leash forward and it snapped abruptly as the dog took off running. He rushed into Mrs. Butler's yard and dived into her flowerbed.

Which word from the paragraph has about the same meaning as *abruptly*?

Ⓐ suddenly

Ⓑ rushed

Ⓒ into

6 Read this sentence from the passage.

> "I could take him into town when I do an errand."

Which sentence from the passage gives a clue about the meaning of *errand*?

Ⓐ "I wish I had a dog with such energy and spirit."

Ⓑ "I would take him to the gardening shop or post office to keep me company."

Ⓒ "I'll walk back to the shelter with you and look into it."

7 Which evidence from the text best supports the theme of the passage?

Ⓐ "Besides being energetic, he's really a sweet and loving dog," said Ana excitedly.

Ⓑ "I've got an idea for your civic leadership project!"

Ⓒ "Helping animals is a cause that is very dear to me."

GO ON →

Read "An Amazing Little Creature" before you answer Numbers 8 through 15.

An Amazing Little Creature

Have you ever seen a hummingbird flying swiftly about? Or maybe you have heard an unusual sound as a hummingbird dives toward a feeder. A hummingbird usually **blares** its arrival. It makes a loud humming noise by fluttering its wings!

Body Structure

A hummingbird moves its wings very quickly at a rate of 38 to 78 beats per second. At times when it is looking for a mate, it can beat its wings as fast as 200 times per second! In addition, a hummingbird is the only bird that can easily fly backward. That is because it uses strong muscles to control its wing movements.

People used to think that hummingbirds were not smart. That is just not the case! Their heads and brains are relatively large for their bodies, so they are able to solve problems. They also have good memories. They can remember exactly where to find the flowers with the most nectar!

A hummingbird's long, slender beak is very useful. It helps the bird poke inside flowers. Then it can get at the nectar that lies deep inside.

A hummingbird's tongue is shaped like a drinking straw. This design allows it to quickly soak up nectar or sugar water from a bird feeder. Imagine licking an ice cream cone. The hummingbird can lick at a rate of 13 licks per second!

GO ON →

Changing Temperatures

Hummingbirds can become **dormant** when the temperature drops outside or when there is little food available. Instead of being active and moving around, hummingbirds sleep. Keeping still allows them to save their energy. This is so that they will not starve.

Hummingbird Migration

When the weather gets cold, food sources are hard to find. Plants and insects begin to die off. So, these little birds migrate toward a warmer climate. They have been known to travel hundreds of miles to find nectar and insects.

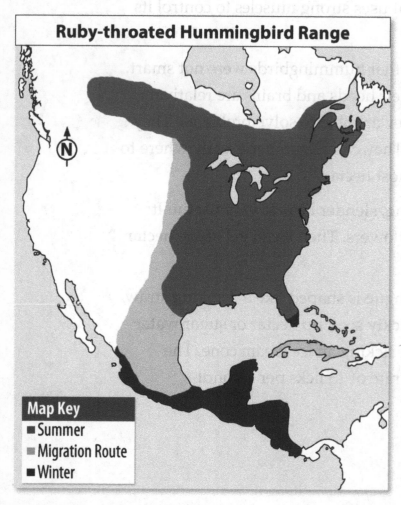

Ruby-throated Hummingbird Range

Map Key
- Summer
- Migration Route
- Winter

The ruby-throated hummingbird travels from North America to Mexico and Central America for winter.

GO ON →

Use "An Amazing Little Creature" to answer Numbers 8 through 15.

8 Read this sentence from the article.

> **A hummingbird usually blares its arrival.**

Which clue words from the article help to explain the meaning of *blares*?

(A) flying swiftly about

(B) making a loud humming noise

(C) fluttering its wings

9 How is a hummingbird able to easily fly backward?

(A) It can beat its wings as fast as 200 times per second.

(B) It uses muscles to control its wing movements.

(C) It tries to keep still to save up its energy.

10 Which feature allows a hummingbird to get at the nectar that lies deep inside flowers?

(A) its strong muscles

(B) its large head

(C) its long beak

GO ON →

11 Hummingbirds can soak up food quickly because they have _____.

Ⓐ small bodies

Ⓑ strong wings

Ⓒ tongues like straws

12 Read these sentences from the article.

Hummingbirds can become dormant when the temperature drops outside or when there is little food available. Instead of being active and moving around, hummingbirds sleep.

Which word from the sentences means the OPPOSITE of *dormant*?

Ⓐ little

Ⓑ active

Ⓒ sleep

13 Which sentence in the text signals a cause-and-effect relationship?

Ⓐ They also have good memories.

Ⓑ This is so that they will not starve.

Ⓒ Plants and insects begin to die off.

GO ON →

14 What problem do hummingbirds face when the weather gets cold?

Ⓐ Food sources become hard to find.

Ⓑ Nectar is hard to get out of flowers.

Ⓒ Their wings do not move as quickly.

15 Which section of the article does the information in the map best support?

Ⓐ Body Structure

Ⓑ Changing Temperatures

Ⓒ Hummingbird Migration

STOP

Fluency Assessment

Paul's Big Problem

Paul Breen felt discouraged. He had been selling fruit, jams, and preserves for a long time. Paul's fruit shop was the best in town. Then a new store, Joy's Veggie Nook, opened up in a small mall nearby. Now Joy seemed to be stealing Paul's customers because his shop had fewer customers each day. He had heard that Joy's store was crowded.

Paul went to talk to Joy. "I am not getting any new customers," he complained. "And the customers I always have had are now coming to you for their healthy snacks."

Joy thought for a moment and then beamed. "I think I can help you out. Why don't we join your fruits with my vegetables? Your shop is roomier than what I have here and can certainly hold two businesses. Customers will buy your fruits, my veggies, and healthy salads from both of us."

Paul thought for a moment. Then he grinned. "We have found the perfect solution!"

What is Paul's problem?

How is the problem solved?

Oral Reading Fluency Assessment

Name: _____ Date: _____

Paul's Big Problem

9	Paul Breen felt discouraged. He had been selling fruit,
20	jams, and preserves for a long time. Paul's fruit shop was
31	the best in town. Then a new store, Joy's Veggie Nook,
43	opened up in a small mall nearby. Now Joy seemed to be
51	stealing Paul's customers because his shop had fewer
60	customers each day. He had heard that Joy's store
62	was crowded.
74	Paul went to talk to Joy. "I am not getting any new
82	customers," he complained. "And the customers I always
93	have had are now coming to you for their healthy snacks."
104	Joy thought for a moment and then beamed. "I think I
116	can help you out. Why don't we join your fruits with my
127	vegetables? Your shop is roomier than what I have here and
136	can certainly hold two businesses. Customers will buy your
146	fruits, my veggies, and healthy salads from both of us."
156	Paul thought for a moment. Then he grinned. "We have
160	found the perfect solution!"

✓ What is Paul's problem?

✓ How is the problem solved?

Words Read	–	Errors	=	WCPM

☐ **Fall (110 WCPM)**
☐ **Winter (127 WCPM)**
☐ **Spring (139 WCPM)**

WCPM	/	Words Read	=	Accuracy %

PROSODY				
	L1	L2	L3	L4
Reading in Phrases	O	O	O	O
Pace	O	O	O	O
Syntax	O	O	O	O
Self-correction	O	O	O	O
Intonation	O	O	O	O

Trees or Gems?

Although both trees and gems are beneficial, or useful, trees are more beneficial. Gems are shiny and pretty. They can be made into necklaces and rings. Hard gems can be used in tools. But trees have even more uses. Trees give us paper and wood. They give us food as well, such as fruit and nuts. Birds and other animals live in trees. Trees also give us air to breathe.

Some people want to protect old trees that are still standing. Others say that aged trees need to be cleared away and young trees planted. The way to solve this argument is to cut only portions of a forest and leave others intact. That saves more trees and creates a healthy forest.

Many think that trees do not need to be protected because they are renewable. But as we cut them, we must replant them. That is the best way to save trees.

✔ Why does the author view trees as important?

✔ In the author's view, what is the best way to save trees?

Name: _____ Date: _____

Trees or Gems?

9	Although both trees and gems are beneficial, or useful,
19	trees are more beneficial. Gems are shiny and pretty. They
30	can be made into necklaces and rings. Hard gems can be
42	used in tools. But trees have even more uses. Trees give us
54	paper and wood. They give us food as well, such as fruit
65	and nuts. Birds and other animals live in trees. Trees also
70	give us air to breathe.
80	Some people want to protect old trees that are still
91	standing. Others say that aged trees need to be cleared away
102	and young trees planted. The way to solve this argument is
114	to cut only portions of a forest and leave others intact. That
122	saves more trees and creates a healthy forest.
132	Many think that trees do not need to be protected
143	because they are renewable. But as we cut them, we must
153	replant them. That is the best way to save trees.

✔ Why does the author view trees as important?

✔ In the author's view, what is the best way to save trees?

Words Read	–	Errors	=	WCPM

☐ **Fall (110 WCPM)**
☐ **Winter (127 WCPM)**
☐ **Spring (139 WCPM)**

WCPM	/	Words Read	=	Accuracy %

PROSODY				
	L1	L2	L3	L4
Reading in Phrases	O	O	O	O
Pace	O	O	O	O
Syntax	O	O	O	O
Self-correction	O	O	O	O
Intonation	O	O	O	O

A Faster Way to Travel

People have always wanted to travel faster. Long ago, people were limited to how fast they could go by their own feet. Then people found that they could travel faster by boat (if there was water nearby). Soon they learned to make canoes and sailboats.

On land, people tamed wild horses. This meant they could ride much faster than they could walk. Yet, they were still limited by how much they could carry. The wheel and the invention of carts and wagons solved this problem. Wagons loaded with goods could be pulled by horses.

Wheels and carts finally led to the invention of trains and cars. Then people could travel much farther. A trip of many months took just a few days. The invention of airplanes made travel even faster. People could travel halfway around the world in a little more than a day. Now people look to the stars. How fast and far can they go in the future?

👆 Name two advances that made travel faster.

👆 Why did people tame wild horses?

Name: _____ Date: _____

A Faster Way to Travel

9	People have always wanted to travel faster. Long ago,
21	people were limited to how fast they could go by their own
32	feet. Then people found that they could travel faster by boat
42	(if there was water nearby). Soon they learned to make
45	canoes and sailboats.
54	On land, people tamed wild horses. This meant they
65	could ride much faster than they could walk. Yet, they were
76	still limited by how much they could carry. The wheel and
85	the invention of carts and wagons solved this problem.
94	Wagons loaded with goods could be pulled by horses.
105	Wheels and carts finally led to the invention of trains and
116	cars. Then people could travel much farther. A trip of many
126	months took just a few days. The invention of airplanes
135	made travel even faster. People could travel halfway around
149	the world in a little more than a day. Now people look to the
160	stars. How fast and far can they go in the future?

✔ Name two advances that made travel faster.

✔ Why did people tame wild horses?

Words Read	–	Errors	=	WCPM

☐ **Fall (110 WCPM)**
☐ **Winter (127 WCPM)**
☐ **Spring (139 WCPM)**

WCPM	/	Words Read	=	Accuracy %

PROSODY				
	L1	L2	L3	L4
Reading in Phrases	O	O	O	O
Pace	O	O	O	O
Syntax	O	O	O	O
Self-correction	O	O	O	O
Intonation	O	O	O	O

Surrender at Yorktown

Jeremy urged his horse to go faster as he raced through the Virginia countryside in 1781. He had heard that General Lord Cornwallis had surrendered to General George Washington in Yorktown. He wondered if the war was nearly over.

Jeremy soon reached his uncle's farm. Bursting through the door, he delivered the momentous news. His uncle made him sit down and take several deep breaths before telling more.

Jeremy had heard the story from a spectator who had watched the ceremony. "He told me that Cornwallis was not there," Jeremy panted. "He pretended to be ill. He sent his second in command instead. The British soldiers were sullen as well. Some threw their weapons down in disgust."

However, the surrender had happened, and it was still surrender. This was a major victory for the American Patriots. But Jeremy and his family would have to wait until 1783 for the Treaty of Paris to be signed. The treaty granted the colonies their independence.

👆 What news does Jeremy have for his uncle?

👆 What text evidence shows that Jeremy is excited?

Name: _____ Date: _____

Surrender at Yorktown

11	Jeremy urged his horse to go faster as he raced through
21	the Virginia countryside in 1781. He had heard that General
28	Lord Cornwallis had surrendered to General George
37	Washington in Yorktown. He wondered if the war was
39	nearly over.
47	Jeremy soon reached his uncle's farm. Bursting through
56	the door, he delivered the momentous news. His uncle
66	made him sit down and take several deep breaths before
68	telling more.
78	Jeremy had heard the story from a spectator who had
88	watched the ceremony. "He told me that Cornwallis was not
99	there," Jeremy panted. "He pretended to be ill. He sent his
108	second in command instead. The British soldiers were sullen
117	as well. Some threw their weapons down in disgust."
126	However, the surrender had happened, and it was still
135	surrender. This was a major victory for the American
146	Patriots. But Jeremy and his family would have to wait until
158	1783 for the Treaty of Paris to be signed. The treaty granted
162	the colonies their independence.

 What news does Jeremy have for his uncle?

 What text evidence shows that Jeremy is excited?

Words Read	–	Errors	=	WCPM

☐ **Fall (110 WCPM)**
☐ **Winter (127 WCPM)**
☐ **Spring (139 WCPM)**

WCPM	/	Words Read	=	Accuracy %

PROSODY

	L1	L2	L3	L4
Reading in Phrases	O	O	O	O
Pace	O	O	O	O
Syntax	O	O	O	O
Self-correction	O	O	O	O
Intonation	O	O	O	O

The Silk Road

The Silk Road was not made of silk. Nor was it truly a road. It was an ancient trade route. The Silk Road linked China and India with the Roman Empire. Silk was just one of the treasures that the caravans, or groups of travelers and traders, carried. They also brought gems, jade, and glass to the West. Horses and exotic foods were traded as well. The caravans returned with Roman gold. Three major routes made up the Silk Road. They snaked across deserts and over mountains for more than 2,800 miles.

Traveling the road was dangerous. Traders had to watch out for bandits who would rob them. There were also tribes who threatened the caravans. Tribal leaders often demanded money. If the traders did not pay, they could not pass.

The Silk Road continued as a major trade route for hundreds of years. More than just a way to sell goods, the Silk Road connected people. The road became a way to exchange new ideas.

👍 Why was the Silk Road important?

👍 How was the Silk Road dangerous?

Name: _____ Date: _____

The Silk Road

13	The Silk Road was not made of silk. Nor was it truly a
24	road. It was an ancient trade route. The Silk Road linked
35	China and India with the Roman Empire. Silk was just one
46	of the treasures that the caravans, or groups of travelers and
56	traders, carried. They also brought gems, jade, and glass to
67	the West. Horses and exotic foods were traded as well. The
75	caravans returned with Roman gold. Three major routes
86	made up the Silk Road. They snaked across deserts and over
92	mountains for more than 2,800 miles.
101	Traveling the road was dangerous. Traders had to watch
112	out for bandits who would rob them. There were also tribes
120	who threatened the caravans. Tribal leaders often demanded
131	money. If the traders did not pay, they could not pass.
141	The Silk Road continued as a major trade route for
153	hundreds of years. More than just a way to sell goods, the
163	Silk Road connected people. The road became a way to
166	exchange new ideas.

✔ Why was the Silk Road important?

✔ How was the Silk Road dangerous?

Words Read	–	Errors	=	WCPM

☐ Fall (110 WCPM)
☐ Winter (127 WCPM)
☐ Spring (139 WCPM)

WCPM	/	Words Read	=	Accuracy %

PROSODY				
	L1	L2	L3	L4
Reading in Phrases	O	O	O	O
Pace	O	O	O	O
Syntax	O	O	O	O
Self-correction	O	O	O	O
Intonation	O	O	O	O

A Living Museum

When the Pilgrims landed on the coast of North America, they did not have homes to move into. They had to build a colony. There were no stores for them to buy food. So they had to grow their own food. They made their own clothing as well.

People today can see what life was like for the pilgrims. They can visit Plimoth Plantation in Massachusetts. An English village has been built here to show people what life was like in 1627. This was only seven years after the colonists arrived. At the time, there were about 160 people living there.

People at the site dress like the colonists did in 1627. They show visitors how the colonists led their daily lives. They also invite visitors to join in activities such as cooking and gardening.

There also are many animals in the village. These are the same types of animals that the colonists had. They include rare breeds of cattle, goats, chickens, and sheep.

✔ What is Plimoth Plantation?

✔ What text evidence shows that life for the Pilgrims was hard?

Name: _____ Date: _____

A Living Museum

10	When the Pilgrims landed on the coast of North America,
23	they did not have homes to move into. They had to build a
35	colony. There were no stores for them to buy food. So they
46	had to grow their own food. They made their own clothing
48	as well.
59	People today can see what life was like for the pilgrims.
67	They can visit Plimoth Plantation in Massachusetts. An
77	English village has been built here to show people what
89	life was like in 1627. This was only seven years after the
99	colonists arrived. At the time, there were about 160 people
101	living there.
112	People at the site dress like the colonists did in 1627.
122	They show visitors how the colonists led their daily lives.
133	They also invite visitors to join in activities such as cooking
135	and gardening.
146	There also are many animals in the village. These are the
156	same types of animals that the colonists had. They include
164	rare breeds of cattle, goats, chickens, and sheep.

✔ What is Plimoth Plantation?

✔ What text evidence shows that life for the Pilgrims was hard?

Words Read	–	Errors	=	WCPM

☐ **Fall (110 WCPM)**
☐ **Winter (127 WCPM)**
☐ **Spring (139 WCPM)**

WCPM	/	Words Read	=	Accuracy %

PROSODY				
	L1	L2	L3	L4
Reading in Phrases	O	O	O	O
Pace	O	O	O	O
Syntax	O	O	O	O
Self-correction	O	O	O	O
Intonation	O	O	O	O

Abigail Rests

Abigail was tired of tending to the herb garden. It was a hot day, and she had been working since early morning. She had fetched water for her mother then fed the chickens. From there she had gone to the garden. Now the sun was high.

Abigail peeked into the small wood-frame house where her mother had just finished baking bread.

"Mother, may I please have a few moments to go to the stream to rest?" Abigail asked. "It is very warm, and I would like some cool water."

Her mother said yes and cautioned her to be careful. Abigail skipped away before her mother could change her mind. She quickly followed the path down to the water where there was shade and a cool place to relax.

Abigail remained for about an hour. She enjoyed listening to the birds' chatter and watching a young deer come for a drink. At last, she felt refreshed. She knew it was time to go back to work.

👆 Why was Abigail tired?

👆 What does Abigail ask her mother?

Name: _____ Date: _____

Abigail Rests

11	Abigail was tired of tending to the herb garden. It was
22	a hot day, and she had been working since early morning.
33	She had fetched water for her mother then fed the chickens.
44	From there she had gone to the garden. Now the sun
46	was high.
55	Abigail peeked into the small wood-frame house where
62	her mother had just finished baking bread.
74	"Mother, may I please have a few moments to go to the
85	stream to rest?" Abigail asked. "It is very warm, and I
90	would like some cool water."
100	Her mother said yes and cautioned her to be careful.
109	Abigail skipped away before her mother could change her
119	mind. She quickly followed the path down to the water
129	where there was shade and a cool place to relax.
138	Abigail remained for about an hour. She enjoyed listening
150	to the birds' chatter and watching a young deer come for a
163	drink. At last, she felt refreshed. She knew it was time to go
166	back to work.

✔ Why was Abigail tired?

✔ What does Abigail ask her mother?

Words Read	–	Errors	=	WCPM

☐ **Fall (110 WCPM)**
☐ **Winter (127 WCPM)**
☐ **Spring (139 WCPM)**

WCPM	/	Words Read	=	Accuracy %

PROSODY				
	L1	L2	L3	L4
Reading in Phrases	O	O	O	O
Pace	O	O	O	O
Syntax	O	O	O	O
Self-correction	O	O	O	O
Intonation	O	O	O	O

A Wildlife Project

Leon's group was having trouble coming up with a topic for its class project. The group had to focus on something local and use some form of technology.

"Let's do local wildlife," Leon said. There was a groan. The group didn't think Leon's idea was interesting at all. The group changed its mind after Leon told more about his idea.

On Saturday, Leon, his classmates, and some adults took a hike. The children used a camera and a cell phone to take pictures and videos. Later, they used a computer to put together their work. They had filmed a close-up of a hawk swooping through the sky. They had pictures of deer, squirrels, and even a fox. There was also a video of a flock of wild turkeys.

The presentation to the class went well. Everyone was surprised at how much wildlife could be seen in the area. They also liked the way the pictures and videos were done. It was more like a movie than a class project.

✔ What problem does Leon's group have?

✔ What does Leon's group do during their hike?

Name: _____ Date: _____

A Wildlife Project

10	Leon's group was having trouble coming up with a topic
21	for its class project. The group had to focus on something
28	local and use some form of technology.
38	"Let's do local wildlife," Leon said. There was a groan.
48	The group didn't think Leon's idea was interesting at all.
58	The group changed its mind after Leon told more about
60	his idea.
69	On Saturday, Leon, his classmates, and some adults took
82	a hike. The children used a camera and a cell phone to take
92	pictures and videos. Later, they used a computer to put
104	together their work. They had filmed a close-up of a hawk
113	swooping through the sky. They had pictures of deer,
126	squirrels, and even a fox. There was also a video of a flock
129	of wild turkeys.
138	The presentation to the class went well. Everyone was
149	surprised at how much wildlife could be seen in the area.
160	They also liked the way the pictures and videos were done.
170	It was more like a movie than a class project.

✔ What problem does Leon's group have?

✔ What does Leon's group do during their hike?

Words Read	–	Errors	=	WCPM

☐ **Fall (110 WCPM)**
☐ **Winter (127 WCPM)**
☐ **Spring (139 WCPM)**

WCPM	/	Words Read	=	Accuracy %

PROSODY				
	L1	L2	L3	L4
Reading in Phrases	O	O	O	O
Pace	O	O	O	O
Syntax	O	O	O	O
Self-correction	O	O	O	O
Intonation	O	O	O	O

Snakes of Many Colors

You might think snakes do not need protection, but they do. Pigs and mongooses prey on snakes. Large birds, such as the serpent eagle, think snakes are good to eat. Even other snakes, such as the King Cobra, hunt other snakes.

Snakes often use color to protect themselves. The bright colors of some snakes warn enemies that the snake is poisonous. Other snakes, such as the Mangrove snake, only pretend to be poisonous. The Pueblan milk snake has bright red, black, and white scales. They are arranged in bands. It looks like another kind of snake that is poisonous. Other animals leave it alone.

Snakes also use their colors to hide themselves. For example, the bright green cat snake lives high in a tree in the rainforest. The snake stays coiled around a branch during the day. It looks just like a vine. This fools animals that might want to make it their dinner.

These snakes need their colorful scales to stay safe. After all, it is a dangerous world—even for a snake.

☑ Why do snakes need protection?

☑ How do snakes use color to help themselves?

Name: _____ Date: _____

Snakes of Many Colors

10	You might think snakes do not need protection, but they
20	do. Pigs and mongooses prey on snakes. Large birds, such
31	as the serpent eagle, think snakes are good to eat. Even
41	other snakes, such as the King Cobra, hunt other snakes.
50	Snakes often use color to protect themselves. The bright
60	colors of some snakes warn enemies that the snake is
69	poisonous. Other snakes, such as the Mangrove snake, only
79	pretend to be poisonous. The Pueblan milk snake has bright
90	red, black, and white scales. They are arranged in bands. It
100	looks like another kind of snake that is poisonous. Other
104	animals leave it alone.
113	Snakes also use their colors to hide themselves. For
126	example, the bright green cat snake lives high in a tree in the
135	rainforest. The snake stays coiled around a branch during
147	the day. It looks just like a vine. This fools animals that
154	might want to make it their dinner.
164	These snakes need their colorful scales to stay safe. After
174	all, it is a dangerous world—even for a snake.

✔ Why do snakes need protection?

✔ How do snakes use color to help themselves?

Words Read	–	Errors	=	WCPM

☐ **Fall (110 WCPM)**
☐ **Winter (127 WCPM)**
☐ **Spring (139 WCPM)**

WCPM	/	Words Read	=	Accuracy %

PROSODY				
	L1	L2	L3	L4
Reading in Phrases	O	O	O	O
Pace	O	O	O	O
Syntax	O	O	O	O
Self-correction	O	O	O	O
Intonation	O	O	O	O

Flying to Help

Pilots fly planes. Some pilots help people in danger by flying to places where people need help. They use their planes to help find people lost in parks. They also dump water and chemicals to put out fires. They bring supplies to the firefighting crew as well.

Pilots need special skills to do their job. For example, pilots who fly to help find people must have fine eyesight. They may have to spot a person from far away. They may have to land in canyons or deep valleys to drop off supplies. Pilots who help to put out fires must be able to respond quickly and focus on safety.

Flying to a fire is dangerous. For example, flames can burn the plane if it flies too low. The air may be filled with smoke, which makes it hard for the pilot to see and breathe.

Flying a plane to put out a fire or to find missing people is not easy. Sometimes it is not safe. But it is a job that helps many people. These brave pilots should be thanked for all they do.

👆 What is the author's view of pilots?

👆 Why is flying to a fire dangerous?

Name: _____ Date: _____

Flying to Help

10	Pilots fly planes. Some pilots help people in danger by
20	flying to places where people need help. They use their
31	planes to help find people lost in parks. They also dump
42	water and chemicals to put out fires. They bring supplies to
47	the firefighting crew as well.
57	Pilots need special skills to do their job. For example,
68	pilots who fly to help find people must have fine eyesight.
80	They may have to spot a person from far away. They may
92	have to land in canyons or deep valleys to drop off supplies.
104	Pilots who help to put out fires must be able to respond
109	quickly and focus on safety.
119	Flying to a fire is dangerous. For example, flames can
133	burn the plane if it flies too low. The air may be filled with
145	smoke, which makes it hard for the pilot to see and breathe.
158	Flying a plane to put out a fire or to find missing people
173	is not easy. Sometimes it is not safe. But it is a job that helps
183	many people. These brave pilots should be thanked for all
185	they do.

✓ What is the author's view of pilots?

✓ Why is flying to a fire dangerous?

Words Read	–	Errors	=	WCPM

☐ **Fall (110 WCPM)**
☐ **Winter (127 WCPM)**
☐ **Spring (139 WCPM)**

WCPM	/	Words Read	=	Accuracy %

PROSODY				
	L1	L2	L3	L4
Reading in Phrases	O	O	O	O
Pace	O	O	O	O
Syntax	O	O	O	O
Self-correction	O	O	O	O
Intonation	O	O	O	O

Victor Discovers History

Victor had no interest in history and did not see any value in learning about the past. "The past is past," he would often proclaim. "I should only be concerned with what is happening now."

One Saturday Victor had nothing to do. He was so bored he decided to take a walk downtown. Around one corner he found a sign that read "Town Museum." He could not imagine what would be in a museum of his town. He did not think there was anything interesting to display. But he went inside to see.

Victor was in the museum for hours. He found out that there had been a rich silver mine near the town in the 1880s, and that there had been a massive explosion which was reported in national newspapers. New safety rules for all mines resulted from the accident.

The town had also been the state capital for a short time right after statehood was granted. This was soon after the railroad had reached the town and new settlers arrived by the hundreds.

"Wow!" Victor said. "I had no idea my town was so amazing!"

👆 How does Victor change in the passage?

👆 Name one thing Victor discovers about his town.

Name: _____ Date: _____

Victor Discovers History

11	Victor had no interest in history and did not see any
22	value in learning about the past. "The past is past," he
31	would often proclaim. "I should only be concerned with
35	what is happening now."
46	One Saturday Victor had nothing to do. He was so bored
57	he decided to take a walk downtown. Around one corner he
67	found a sign that read "Town Museum." He could not
79	imagine what would be in a museum of his town. He did
89	not think there was anything interesting to display. But he
93	went inside to see.
104	Victor was in the museum for hours. He found out that
117	there had been a rich silver mine near the town in the 1880s,
127	and that there had been a massive explosion which was
136	reported in national newspapers. New safety rules for all
141	mines resulted from the accident.
153	The town had also been the state capital for a short time
163	right after statehood was granted. This was soon after the
173	railroad had reached the town and new settlers arrived by
175	the hundreds.
185	"Wow!" Victor said. "I had no idea my town was
187	so amazing!"

 How does Victor change in the passage?

 Name one thing Victor discovers about his town.

Words Read	–	Errors	=	WCPM

☐ **Fall (110 WCPM)**
☐ **Winter (127 WCPM)**
☐ **Spring (139 WCPM)**

WCPM	/	Words Read	=	Accuracy %

PROSODY				
	L1	L2	L3	L4
Reading in Phrases	O	O	O	O
Pace	O	O	O	O
Syntax	O	O	O	O
Self-correction	O	O	O	O
Intonation	O	O	O	O

Super Spots

A leopard has spots for more than one reason. The leopard's spots are dark brown and shaped like flowers. They help the big cat hide from its prey. In forests and grasslands, the spots break up the shape of the leopard. Other animals cannot easily see the leopard.

Another reason for the spots is communication. A leopard has a white spot on the tip of its tail and on the backs of its ears. These spots help leopards find each other in tall grass.

Even black leopards have spots. These cats live in the dark rain forests of Southeast Asia. They look solid black. But their spots can be seen from the right angle.

Jaguars and cheetahs are other big cats with spots. The spots of all three cats are about the same color. But the spots are different shapes. Jaguar spots are also like flowers, but they are bigger than leopard spots. Jaguar spots also have dots in the center. Cheetahs have solid spots that are evenly spread across its body.

How do leopards use spots to communicate?

What is the major difference between the spots of big cats?

Name: _____ Date: _____

Super Spots

10	A leopard has spots for more than one reason. The
19	leopard's spots are dark brown and shaped like flowers.
31	They help the big cat hide from its prey. In forests and
41	grasslands, the spots break up the shape of the leopard.
48	Other animals cannot easily see the leopard.
57	Another reason for the spots is communication. A leopard
73	has a white spot on the tip of its tail and on the backs of its
84	ears. These spots help leopards find each other in tall grass.
94	Even black leopards have spots. These cats live in the
104	dark rain forests of Southeast Asia. They look solid black.
114	But their spots can be seen from the right angle.
124	Jaguars and cheetahs are other big cats with spots. The
137	spots of all three cats are about the same color. But the spots
147	are different shapes. Jaguar spots are also like flowers, but
157	they are bigger than leopard spots. Jaguar spots also have
168	dots in the center. Cheetahs have solid spots that are evenly
172	spread across its body.

✔ How do leopards use spots to communicate?

✔ What is the major difference between the spots of big cats?

Words Read	–	Errors	=	WCPM

☐ **Fall (110 WCPM)**
☐ **Winter (127 WCPM)**
☐ **Spring (139 WCPM)**

WCPM	/	Words Read	=	Accuracy %

PROSODY	L1	L2	L3	L4
Reading in Phrases	O	O	O	O
Pace	O	O	O	O
Syntax	O	O	O	O
Self-correction	O	O	O	O
Intonation	O	O	O	O

Rare Air

You can't see it, but clean air is an important and often rare resource. Nearly every living thing needs air to live. If air becomes dirty because of pollution, plants can die. People and animals can become sick.

Air pollution is often from smoke. In the 1200s in England, people complained about smoke when coal was first burned. Today, people burn oil and natural gas to heat their homes and operate their cars. Air pollution also comes from businesses, such as electrical plants.

When you can see hazy brown air, you know that it's dirty. Polluted air traps gases. When these gases cannot escape, they raise the temperature of Earth. People cannot breathe easily when the air is bad. Their eyes become red, and noses and lungs are irritated. They can develop asthma and other breathing problems.

There are ways to control air pollution. But they are costly. Many businesses do not want to pay a lot of money. Customers do not want to pay more for the products they buy.

👆 Why is clean air important?

👆 What problem does the author point out about controlling air pollution?

Name: _____ Date: _____

Rare Air

12	You can't see it, but clean air is an important and often
22	rare resource. Nearly every living thing needs air to live.
32	If air becomes dirty because of pollution, plants can die.
38	People and animals can become sick.
48	Air pollution is often from smoke. In the 1200s in
56	England, people complained about smoke when coal was
67	first burned. Today, people burn oil and natural gas to heat
77	their homes and operate their cars. Air pollution also comes
83	from businesses, such as electrical plants.
94	When you can see hazy brown air, you know that it's
103	dirty. Polluted air traps gases. When these gases cannot
112	escape, they raise the temperature of Earth. People cannot
123	breathe easily when the air is bad. Their eyes become red,
133	and noses and lungs are irritated. They can develop asthma
137	and other breathing problems.
147	There are ways to control air pollution. But they are
159	costly. Many businesses do not want to pay a lot of money.
169	Customers do not want to pay more for the products
171	they buy.

✔ Why is clean air important?

✔ What problem does the author point out about controlling air pollution?

Words Read	–	Errors	=	WCPM

- ☐ **Fall (110 WCPM)**
- ☐ **Winter (127 WCPM)**
- ☐ **Spring (139 WCPM)**

WCPM	/	Words Read	=	Accuracy %

PROSODY				
	L1	L2	L3	L4
Reading in Phrases	O	O	O	O
Pace	O	O	O	O
Syntax	O	O	O	O
Self-correction	O	O	O	O
Intonation	O	O	O	O

Bright Stars

The Bayville Bright Stars played baseball, but none of them were stars. Each player had been rejected by another, better team.

The Bayville Bright Stars were definitely a team. The players liked each other, and they worked well together. As they organized their team, they discovered that each team member had one skill. Shawn could run fast while José could throw a baseball a long distance. Taylor was capable of watching the whole field to see what everyone was doing. Vera was good at shortstop; this was the one position she could play well. None of the Bright Stars were excellent players, but they were consistently good. Best of all, the team loved to play baseball.

The team decided to let each player choose his best position. They practiced often until their first game was scheduled. They didn't win that game, but at least they scored.

In the last game of the season, the Bright Stars finally demonstrated what they could do. They beat the best team by one run and shocked everyone. No team could have been happier with a win.

✔ How were the Bayville Bright Stars formed?

✔ Why does the narrator believe the Bayville Bright Stars are a good team?

Name: _____ Date: _____

Bright Stars

9	The Bayville Bright Stars played baseball, but none of
19	them were stars. Each player had been rejected by another,
21	better team.
30	The Bayville Bright Stars were definitely a team. The
40	players liked each other, and they worked well together. As
49	they organized their team, they discovered that each team
59	member had one skill. Shawn could run fast while José
69	could throw a baseball a long distance. Taylor was capable
79	of watching the whole field to see what everyone was
90	doing. Vera was good at shortstop; this was the one position
101	she could play well. None of the Bright Stars were excellent
111	players, but they were consistently good. Best of all, the
116	team loved to play baseball.
126	The team decided to let each player choose his best
134	position. They practiced often until their first game
144	was scheduled. They didn't win that game, but at least
146	they scored.
157	In the last game of the season, the Bright Stars finally
167	demonstrated what they could do. They beat the best team
178	by one run and shocked everyone. No team could have been
182	happier with a win.

✔ How were the Bayville Bright Stars formed?

✔ Why does the narrator believe the Bayville Bright Stars are a good team?

Words Read	–	Errors	=	WCPM

☐ **Fall (110 WCPM)**
☐ **Winter (127 WCPM)**
☐ **Spring (139 WCPM)**

WCPM	/	Words Read	=	Accuracy %

PROSODY				
	L1	L2	L3	L4
Reading in Phrases	O	O	O	O
Pace	O	O	O	O
Syntax	O	O	O	O
Self-correction	O	O	O	O
Intonation	O	O	O	O

The Hidden Door

Zoe and Carl thought their new home was the oddest place. The big, rambling house squatted like a toad in the middle of a large field. It had been built in the mid-1800s as part of a large farm. It had many rooms and wandering hallways. Sometimes a hall would come to an abrupt stop. Stairs ended at a solid wall.

After several weeks, Zoe and Carl thought they knew everything about the old house. But their parents had one more surprise.

"Have you found the hidden door in the library?" their father asked.

The twins gazed around the room, seeing only tall shelves filled with books. Their father walked over to one bookcase and reached up under a shelf. They heard a click, and a part of the bookcase moved forward. There was a door behind it.

"We've discovered that this house used to be a part of the Underground Railroad before the Civil War. Escaped slaves from the South would stay in the rooms behind this bookcase. No one would find them behind the hidden door," the twins' mother explained.

👆 What is the house's biggest surprise?

👆 How is the house a part of history?

Name: _____   Date: _____

The Hidden Door

10	Zoe and Carl thought their new home was the oddest
21	place. The big, rambling house squatted like a toad in the
34	middle of a large field. It had been built in the mid-1800s as
45	part of a large farm. It had many rooms and wandering
55	hallways. Sometimes a hall would come to an abrupt stop.
61	Stairs ended at a solid wall.
70	After several weeks, Zoe and Carl thought they knew
80	everything about the old house. But their parents had one
82	more surprise.
92	"Have you found the hidden door in the library?" their
94	father asked.
103	The twins gazed around the room, seeing only tall
113	shelves filled with books. Their father walked over to one
124	bookcase and reached up under a shelf. They heard a click,
135	and a part of the bookcase moved forward. There was a
138	door behind it.
150	"We've discovered that this house used to be a part of the
158	Underground Railroad before the Civil War. Escaped slaves
168	from the South would stay in the rooms behind this
177	bookcase. No one would find them behind the hidden
182	door," the twins' mother explained.

 What is the house's biggest surprise?

 How is the house a part of history?

Words Read	–	Errors	=	WCPM

☐ **Fall (110 WCPM)**
☐ **Winter (127 WCPM)**
☐ **Spring (139 WCPM)**

WCPM	/	Words Read	=	Accuracy %

PROSODY				
	L1	**L2**	**L3**	**L4**
Reading in Phrases	O	O	O	O
Pace	O	O	O	O
Syntax	O	O	O	O
Self-correction	O	O	O	O
Intonation	O	O	O	O

A Closer Look

Megan felt as though she had landed on another planet. She was spending the summer with her aunt and uncle who lived on a large ranch in Wyoming. Megan had come from a busy city in California.

On her first day, Megan went outside and gazed at the landscape. The land seemed completely empty as it stretched for miles.

"There's nothing here," Megan complained.

"Just wait," her aunt said and smiled.

Megan did wait, but nothing seemed to happen. Then one day, Megan's aunt and uncle took her for a ride to a mountain meadow where Megan saw beautiful wildflowers, but that was all.

And then over the wildflowers flitted tiny hummingbirds. Their wings moved in a blur. Megan's aunt explained that they were Rufous hummingbirds. Then she pointed up in the sky where Megan saw a mass of fluttering insects. They turned out to be Monarch butterflies migrating to Wyoming from their winter home in Mexico.

"In the fall the elk herds migrate," Megan's uncle said. "There is always something to see if you look closer."

✔ What is Megan's problem at the start of the passage?

✔ What lesson does Megan learn?

Name: _____ Date: _____

A Closer Look

10	Megan felt as though she had landed on another planet.
21	She was spending the summer with her aunt and uncle who
33	lived on a large ranch in Wyoming. Megan had come from a
37	busy city in California.
48	On her first day, Megan went outside and gazed at the
56	landscape. The land seemed completely empty as it
59	stretched for miles.
64	"There's nothing here," Megan complained.
71	"Just wait," her aunt said and smiled.
80	Megan did wait, but nothing seemed to happen. Then
93	one day, Megan's aunt and uncle took her for a ride to a
100	mountain meadow where Megan saw beautiful wildflowers,
104	but that was all.
112	And then over the wildflowers flitted tiny hummingbirds.
122	Their wings moved in a blur. Megan's aunt explained that
131	they were Rufous hummingbirds. Then she pointed up in
142	the sky where Megan saw a mass of fluttering insects. They
151	turned out to be Monarch butterflies migrating to Wyoming
157	from their winter home in Mexico.
167	"In the fall the elk herds migrate," Megan's uncle said.
177	"There is always something to see if you look closer."

 What is Megan's problem at the start of the passage?

 What lesson does Megan learn?

Words Read	–	Errors	=	WCPM

☐ **Fall (110 WCPM)**
☐ **Winter (127 WCPM)**
☐ **Spring (139 WCPM)**

WCPM	/	Words Read	=	Accuracy %

PROSODY	L1	L2	L3	L4
Reading in Phrases	O	O	O	O
Pace	O	O	O	O
Syntax	O	O	O	O
Self-correction	O	O	O	O
Intonation	O	O	O	O

The Seashore

There are many fun activities to choose from when you visit the seashore. The beaches, boardwalks, and ocean waters offer many things to do. You can build sandcastles, swim, surf, collect shells, or play games.

Lots of people like to collect seashells. Miles of sandy shores invite a walk along the water's edge. You will find that the waves push many shells onto the sand. Soft-bodied sea animals, called mollusks, use these shells for protection.

The ocean can cool you off on a hot day. Swimming and surfing are two ways to enjoy the water. Riding waves on a surfboard can be lots of fun! However, it is important for swimmers and surfers to be careful. Big waves or strong tides can make a fun activity unsafe.

If you like to play games, be sure to visit the beach and boardwalk. You can join a beach ballgame. You can also watch and cheer on the players. Most boardwalk games cost money but offer prizes if you win.

Paid passes are needed on many beaches. Often you can prepay for a whole season of fun. Then you can return to the seashore anytime. Everyone should go to the seashore!

What is the author's view of the seashore?

What are mollusks?

Name: _____ Date: _____

The Seashore

10	There are many fun activities to choose from when you
18	visit the seashore. The beaches, boardwalks, and ocean
28	waters offer many things to do. You can build sandcastles,
35	swim, surf, collect shells, or play games.
45	Lots of people like to collect seashells. Miles of sandy
56	shores invite a walk along the water's edge. You will find
67	that the waves push many shells onto the sand. Soft-bodied
76	sea animals, called mollusks, use these shells for protection.
88	The ocean can cool you off on a hot day. Swimming and
100	surfing are two ways to enjoy the water. Riding waves on a
111	surfboard can be lots of fun! However, it is important for
121	swimmers and surfers to be careful. Big waves or strong
128	tides can make a fun activity unsafe.
141	If you like to play games, be sure to visit the beach and
151	boardwalk. You can join a beach ballgame. You can also
161	watch and cheer on the players. Most boardwalk games cost
168	money but offer prizes if you win.
178	Paid passes are needed on many beaches. Often you can
191	prepay for a whole season of fun. Then you can return to the
199	seashore anytime. Everyone should go to the seashore!

✔ What is the author's view of the seashore?

✔ What are mollusks?

Words Read	–	Errors	=	WCPM

☐ **Fall (110 WCPM)**
☐ **Winter (127 WCPM)**
☐ **Spring (139 WCPM)**

WCPM	/	Words Read	=	Accuracy %

PROSODY				
	L1	L2	L3	L4
Reading in Phrases	O	O	O	O
Pace	O	O	O	O
Syntax	O	O	O	O
Self-correction	O	O	O	O
Intonation	O	O	O	O

Alicia's Dilemma

Alicia had a dog, a miniature schnauzer named Rosie that she had grown up with. Now Alicia had a little sister, Marta, who also loved the dog. But Marta was always sick with red, itchy eyes and a runny nose. Lately, she was getting ear infections.

"Your sister is allergic to your pooch," Dr. Hurtago said to Alicia one day when her mom had taken Marta to the doctor's office.

"Rosie is a member of our family," said Alicia's mom. "But Marta cannot be sick all the time."

The girls went home and embraced Rosie, which caused Marta to start sniffling all over again.

The next day after school, Alicia went to see Rosie's veterinarian. "I love Rosie, but she can't stay with us. She needs another home; it has to be someplace where I could visit her," Alicia explained.

The vet looked thoughtfully at her. "My sister loves schnauzers, and she just moved into town. She has been thinking about getting a dog, so this may be perfect."

"Could I visit and take Rosie for walks?" Alicia asked.

"I'm sure you could," said the vet with a smile.

✔ What is Alicia's dilemma?

✔ How does the veterinarian help Alicia?

Oral Reading Fluency Assessment

Name: _____ Date: _____

Alicia's Dilemma

10	Alicia had a dog, a miniature schnauzer named Rosie that
22	she had grown up with. Now Alicia had a little sister, Marta,
33	who also loved the dog. But Marta was always sick with
44	red, itchy eyes and a runny nose. Lately, she was getting
46	ear infections.
56	"Your sister is allergic to your pooch," Dr. Hurtago said
68	to Alicia one day when her mom had taken Marta to the
70	doctor's office.
80	"Rosie is a member of our family," said Alicia's mom.
88	"But Marta cannot be sick all the time."
97	The girls went home and embraced Rosie, which caused
104	Marta to start sniffling all over again.
114	The next day after school, Alicia went to see Rosie's
125	veterinarian. "I love Rosie, but she can't stay with us. She
136	needs another home; it has to be someplace where I could
140	visit her," Alicia explained.
149	The vet looked thoughtfully at her. "My sister loves
159	schnauzers, and she just moved into town. She has been
169	thinking about getting a dog, so this may be perfect."
179	"Could I visit and take Rosie for walks?" Alicia asked.
189	"I'm sure you could," said the vet with a smile.

✓ What is Alicia's dilemma?

✓ How does the veterinarian help Alicia?

Words Read	–	Errors	=	WCPM

☐ **Fall (110 WCPM)**
☐ **Winter (127 WCPM)**
☐ **Spring (139 WCPM)**

WCPM	/	Words Read	=	Accuracy %

PROSODY				
	L1	L2	L3	L4
Reading in Phrases	O	O	O	O
Pace	O	O	O	O
Syntax	O	O	O	O
Self-correction	O	O	O	O
Intonation	O	O	O	O

Making Perfume

Lin loved the smell of flowers and forest pine needles. She loved the smell of oranges and lemons.

Lin wondered how people made perfumes and got smells out of things in nature. So her mother took her to a perfume factory to see. A tour guide told them many things about perfumes.

The guide said that perfumes are made from oils. The oils once came from flowers, leaves, fruits, roots, and seeds. Oils from these sources are still used. But scientists can now make many of the same smells in their labs. They also make new smells that are not found in nature.

Lin watched people extracting oils. Some oils were squeezed out while others were boiled out. Some people were putting flower petals on big, flat trays. They covered the petals with pork fat that could pull out the sweet smells.

The guide said that as many as 300 different smells can go into one perfume. People who make perfumes must have a good sense of smell. They must also know how to put different smells together.

Lin thought about her sense of smell. She wondered if some day she might be able to make perfumes.

👆 Why does Lin's mother take her to the factory?

👆 How can smells that are not found in nature be found in perfumes?

Name: _____ Date: _____

Making Perfume

10	Lin loved the smell of flowers and forest pine needles.
18	She loved the smell of oranges and lemons.
26	Lin wondered how people made perfumes and got
39	smells out of things in nature. So her mother took her to a
50	perfume factory to see. A tour guide told them many things
52	about perfumes.
63	The guide said that perfumes are made from oils. The oils
73	once came from flowers, leaves, fruits, roots, and seeds. Oils
83	from these sources are still used. But scientists can now
95	make many of the same smells in their labs. They also make
103	new smells that are not found in nature.
111	Lin watched people extracting oils. Some oils were
120	squeezed out while others were boiled out. Some people
130	were putting flower petals on big, flat trays. They covered
142	the petals with pork fat that could pull out the sweet smells.
153	The guide said that as many as 300 different smells can
163	go into one perfume. People who make perfumes must have
175	a good sense of smell. They must also know how to put
178	different smells together.
188	Lin thought about her sense of smell. She wondered if
197	some day she might be able to make perfumes.

✓ Why does Lin's mother take her to the factory?

✓ How can smells that are not found in nature be found in perfumes?

Words Read	–	Errors	=	WCPM

☐ **Fall (110 WCPM)**
☐ **Winter (127 WCPM)**
☐ **Spring (139 WCPM)**

WCPM	/	Words Read	=	Accuracy %

PROSODY	L1	L2	L3	L4
Reading in Phrases	O	O	O	O
Pace	O	O	O	O
Syntax	O	O	O	O
Self-correction	O	O	O	O
Intonation	O	O	O	O

Carrie Chapman Catt

Women and men in the United States did not always share a right to vote. Men were in charge of voting, and women had no role in government. Susan B. Anthony tried to change the law. She fought hard for women's right to vote. This did not happen while Anthony was alive.

A woman named Carrie Chapman Catt joined Susan B. Anthony in the fight for women's rights. Catt was offended by the way women were treated. She felt that granting women the right to vote could not be delayed any longer.

Catt became part of a woman's group that discussed such topics as peace and women's rights. Catt told the group that women must have a part in making decisions. So she started a plan to bring women together. The women recognized that Catt was smart and her speeches were convincing. They agreed to help.

Catt organized marches and got women to write letters. This helped them reach many others. Several states began to allow women to vote. Finally, in 1920, women were granted the right to vote by the United States government. They had won their fight, and Catt had made a mark on history.

👆 What did Catt work to achieve?

👆 How did Catt convince other women to join her cause?

Name: _____ Date: _____

Carrie Chapman Catt

10	Women and men in the United States did not always
22	share a right to vote. Men were in charge of voting, and
32	women had no role in government. Susan B. Anthony tried
43	to change the law. She fought hard for women's right to
52	vote. This did not happen while Anthony was alive.
61	A woman named Carrie Chapman Catt joined Susan B.
71	Anthony in the fight for women's rights. Catt was offended
81	by the way women were treated. She felt that granting
92	women the right to vote could not be delayed any longer.
101	Catt became part of a woman's group that discussed
111	such topics as peace and women's rights. Catt told the
121	group that women must have a part in making decisions.
132	So she started a plan to bring women together. The women
141	recognized that Catt was smart and her speeches were
146	convincing. They agreed to help.
155	Catt organized marches and got women to write letters.
165	This helped them reach many others. Several states began to
175	allow women to vote. Finally, in 1920, women were granted
186	the right to vote by the United States government. They had
197	won their fight, and Catt had made a mark on history.

✔ What did Catt work to achieve?

✔ How did Catt convince other women to join her cause?

Words Read	–	Errors	=	WCPM

☐ **Fall (110 WCPM)**
☐ **Winter (127 WCPM)**
☐ **Spring (139 WCPM)**

WCPM	/	Words Read	=	Accuracy %

PROSODY				
	L1	L2	L3	L4
Reading in Phrases	O	O	O	O
Pace	O	O	O	O
Syntax	O	O	O	O
Self-correction	O	O	O	O
Intonation	O	O	O	O

Changing Views of Earth

As you watch the moon and stars at night or see the sun rise and set, it's easy to imagine that the sky revolves around Earth. This was what people long ago thought. They believed that Earth was the center of the universe.

When some ancient Greek astronomers suggested that Earth revolved around the sun, others thought this idea was wrong. Astronomers long ago did not have telescopes to prove their ideas.

In the 1500s and 1600s, astronomers began to use telescopes, which had been invented by the Dutch. Galileo Gallilei was one of the most famous of these astronomers. He believed his observations of the skies proved that Earth revolved around the sun. He had seen moons orbiting the planet Jupiter. So he knew that not everything in space circled Earth. Galileo was criticized for his ideas. Many people were not ready to accept that Earth did not have the most important place in the universe.

As years passed, astronomers had better equipment. They also said that Earth orbited the sun. At last, everyone had to agree. The proof was too strong. And then a new idea was proposed. The sun was not the center of the universe, either!

👆 What did people long ago believe about Earth?

👆 How did telescopes affect people's views about the universe?

Name: _____ Date: _____

Changing Views of the Earth

13	As you watch the moon and stars at night or see the sun
24	rise and set, it's easy to imagine that the sky revolves
34	around Earth. This was what people long ago thought. They
43	believed that Earth was the center of the universe.
50	When some ancient Greek astronomers suggested that
60	Earth revolved around the sun, others thought this idea was
69	wrong. Astronomers long ago did not have telescopes to
72	prove their ideas.
81	In the 1500s and 1600s, astronomers began to use
90	telescopes, which had been invented by the Dutch. Galileo
100	Gallilei was one of the most famous of these astronomers.
110	He believed his observations of the skies proved that Earth
120	revolved around the sun. He had seen moons orbiting the
130	planet Jupiter. So he knew that not everything in space
139	circled Earth. Galileo was criticized for his ideas. Many
151	people were not ready to accept that Earth did not have the
157	most important place in the universe.
164	As years passed, astronomers had better equipment.
175	They also said that Earth orbited the sun. At last, everyone
187	had to agree. The proof was too strong. And then a new
198	idea was proposed. The sun was not the center of the
200	universe, either!

✔ What did people long ago believe about Earth?

✔ How did telescopes affect people's views about the universe?

Words Read	–	Errors	=	WCPM

☐ **Fall (110 WCPM)**
☐ **Winter (127 WCPM)**
☐ **Spring (139 WCPM)**

WCPM	/	Words Read	=	Accuracy %

PROSODY				
	L1	L2	L3	L4
Reading in Phrases	O	O	O	O
Pace	O	O	O	O
Syntax	O	O	O	O
Self-correction	O	O	O	O
Intonation	O	O	O	O

The Bridge

Once there was a village that was nestled high in the mountains. The only way to reach the village was to cross a rushing river and travel up a steep and rocky path that twisted around the mountains. The river was dangerous. The path was narrow and difficult to walk on, but the villagers liked it that way. The villagers did not welcome strangers, although they were polite when one arrived. And the world went on, leaving the village behind.

One day gold was discovered in the mountains around the village. Suddenly, strangers were everywhere, climbing the steep path and digging into the mountainsides. Many miners were hurt as they looked for gold. They fell from the path and slid down the mountain. They became lost in the path's twists and turns. Some disappeared and were never seen again.

At last, people in the valleys decided they must build a bridge across the river and make the path straight. When it was finished, the path to the village and into the mountains was much safer. New people came and moved into the village. They built homes and started businesses. The world had arrived, and the village was forever changed.

✓ How does the discovery of gold change the village?

✓ Why do the people in the valleys build a bridge?

Name: _____ Date: _____

The Bridge

11	Once there was a village that was nestled high in the
23	mountains. The only way to reach the village was to cross a
34	rushing river and travel up a steep and rocky path that
42	twisted around the mountains. The river was dangerous.
53	The path was narrow and difficult to walk on, but the
63	villagers liked it that way. The villagers did not welcome
72	strangers, although they were polite when one arrived. And
80	the world went on, leaving the village behind.
89	One day gold was discovered in the mountains around
96	the village. Suddenly, strangers were everywhere, climbing
105	the steep path and digging into the mountainsides. Many
117	miners were hurt as they looked for gold. They fell from the
128	path and slid down the mountain. They became lost in the
137	path's twists and turns. Some disappeared and were never
139	seen again.
150	At last, people in the valleys decided they must build a
161	bridge across the river and make the path straight. When it
172	was finished, the path to the village and into the mountains
182	was much safer. New people came and moved into the
191	village. They built homes and started businesses. The world
199	had arrived, and the village was forever changed.

✔ How does the discovery of gold change the village?

✔ Why do the people in the valleys build a bridge?

Words Read	–	Errors	=	WCPM

☐ **Fall (110 WCPM)**
☐ **Winter (127 WCPM)**
☐ **Spring (139 WCPM)**

WCPM	/	Words Read	=	Accuracy %

PROSODY				
	L1	L2	L3	L4
Reading in Phrases	O	O	O	O
Pace	O	O	O	O
Syntax	O	O	O	O
Self-correction	O	O	O	O
Intonation	O	O	O	O

Seed Treasures

Many people think of treasure as gold, silver, and precious gems. However, gardeners know that their treasure is seeds. They especially value seeds that are known as *heirlooms*.

An heirloom is something valuable. It is handed down from generation to generation. Heirloom seeds come from plants that people have been growing for a long time. Some heirloom plants were first cultivated by Native Americans hundreds of years ago.

Besides age, heirloom seeds are thought to be "true-to-type." This means that the seeds will produce a plant like the one they came from. Most vegetables grown today are from hybrid plants. The seeds from these plants are often not true-to-type. They may not even grow. If they do, the vegetables often are not like those that came from the parent plant.

Many gardeners also like heirloom seeds because of quality. These gardeners want tomatoes that taste like real tomatoes. They do not want tomatoes that taste like something else. They want sweet and juicy corn. They do not want something that looks good but has little taste.

👆 What are heirloom seeds?

👆 Why are heirloom seeds considered "true-to-type"?

Name: _____ Date: _____

Seed Treasures

9	Many people think of treasure as gold, silver, and
16	precious gems. However, gardeners know that their
25	treasure is seeds. They especially value seeds that are
28	known as *heirlooms*.
37	An heirloom is something valuable. It is handed down
45	from generation to generation. Heirloom seeds come from
56	plants that people have been growing for a long time. Some
64	heirloom plants were first cultivated by Native Americans
68	hundreds of years ago.
78	Besides age, heirloom seeds are thought to be "true-to-
89	type." This means that the seeds will produce a plant like
99	the one they came from. Most vegetables grown today are
109	from hybrid plants. The seeds from these plants are often
122	not true-to-type. They may not even grow. If they do, the
132	vegetables often are not like those that came from the
134	parent plant.
142	Many gardeners also like heirloom seeds because of
151	quality. These gardeners want tomatoes that taste like real
160	tomatoes. They do not want tomatoes that taste like
170	something else. They want sweet and juicy corn. They do
180	not want something that looks good but has little taste.

 What are heirloom seeds?

 Why are heirloom seeds considered "true-to-type"?

Words Read	–	Errors	=	WCPM

☐ **Fall (110 WCPM)**
☐ **Winter (127 WCPM)**
☐ **Spring (139 WCPM)**

WCPM	/	Words Read	=	Accuracy %

PROSODY				
	L1	L2	L3	L4
Reading in Phrases	O	O	O	O
Pace	O	O	O	O
Syntax	O	O	O	O
Self-correction	O	O	O	O
Intonation	O	O	O	O

The Fox

The sun was about to set, so the fennec fox knew that it was about time to hunt for food. He poked his nose out of his underground den. Then his whole head emerged.

Anyone watching might think that a much larger animal lived there. The fox's ears were at least half the length of his 12-inch body. The fox treasured his ears because they helped to keep him cool in the searing desert heat. He also was proud of his long, thick hair. It also protected him from the hot sun and kept him warm at night. *It looks good, too*, the fox thought.

Out on the sand, the fox roamed. He was not picky about food. He would eat plants, rodents, eggs, small reptiles, and insects. If he found water, he might drink some, but he did not need it. He could survive without water for a long time.

At last, the fox sensed a reptile nest. He used his hairy feet to dig up the eggs. He finished his tasty meal before the other foxes in his community found out he had a wonderful treat. Then it was back to his cool den under the sand as the sun began to rise.

Why does the fox think highly of his ears?

Why does the fox not search for water?

Name: _____ Date: _____

The Fox

13	The sun was about to set, so the fennec fox knew that it
26	was about time to hunt for food. He poked his nose out of
34	his underground den. Then his whole head emerged.
43	Anyone watching might think that a much larger animal
56	lived there. The fox's ears were at least half the length of his
66	12-inch body. The fox treasured his ears because they helped
78	to keep him cool in the searing desert heat. He also was
90	proud of his long, thick hair. It also protected him from the
103	hot sun and kept him warm at night. *It looks good, too*, the
105	fox thought.
117	Out on the sand, the fox roamed. He was not picky about
127	food. He would eat plants, rodents, eggs, small reptiles, and
139	insects. If he found water, he might drink some, but he did
151	not need it. He could survive without water for a long time.
163	At last, the fox sensed a reptile nest. He used his hairy
176	feet to dig up the eggs. He finished his tasty meal before the
187	other foxes in his community found out he had a wonderful
201	treat. Then it was back to his cool den under the sand as the
205	sun began to rise.

✔ Why does the fox think highly of his ears?

✔ Why does the fox not search for water?

Words Read	–	Errors	=	WCPM

☐ **Fall (110 WCPM)**
☐ **Winter (127 WCPM)**
☐ **Spring (139 WCPM)**

WCPM	/	Words Read	=	Accuracy %

PROSODY				
	L1	L2	L3	L4
Reading in Phrases	O	O	O	O
Pace	O	O	O	O
Syntax	O	O	O	O
Self-correction	O	O	O	O
Intonation	O	O	O	O

Scoring Sheets and Answer Keys

Name: _____ Date: _____

WEEKLY ASSESSMENT SCORING SHEET   UNIT __ WEEK __

Item	Content Focus	Score	Comments
1			
2			
3			
4			
5			

Assessment · Scoring Sheet

Name: _____ Date: _____

MID-UNIT SCORING SHEET   UNIT __

Item	Content Focus	Score	Comments
1			
2			
3			
4			
5			
6			
7			
8			
9			
10			

Name: _____ Date: _____

UNIT ASSESSMENT SCORING SHEET   UNIT ___

Item	Content Focus	Score	Comments
1			
2			
3			
4			
5			
6			
7			
8			
9			
10			
11			
12			
13			
14			
15			

Name: _____ Date: _____

EXIT ASSESSMENT SCORING SHEET   UNIT __

Item	Content Focus	Score	Comments
1			
2			
3			
4			
5			
6			
7			
8			
9			
10			
11			
12			
13			
14			
15			

Weekly Assessment Answer Key

UNIT 1 WEEK 1

Item #	Content Focus
1	Vocabulary: Context Clues
2	Sequence
3	Vocabulary: Context Clues
4	Sequence
5	Sequence

Suggested Responses:

1 **Text Evidence:** piggy bank was empty; at a real bank
money that is saved

2 **Text Evidence:** Maybe they would pay Cam to walk their dogs after school.
She puts up signs around the neighborhood.

3 **Text Evidence:** Cam earned a lot of money
be able to pay for

4 **Text Evidence:** As she headed down the street, she tripped over the leashes.

5 **Text Evidence:** "I can help on Tuesday and Thursday," said Alice. "I can help on Wednesday and Friday," said Clara.
Alice

UNIT 1 WEEK 2

Item #	Content Focus
1	Vocabulary: Context Clues
2	Problem and Solution
3	Problem and Solution
4	Vocabulary: Context Clues
5	Problem and Solution

Suggested Responses:

1 **Text Evidence:** "It will take a while to make new friends," I thought. The worst part was that I would have to leave my best friend, Ahmed.
nervous

2 He does not want to move to the city.
Text Evidence: I did not want to move!

3 He tries to talk to his mother about his fears.

4 **Text Evidence:** she did not pay attention; she was busy rushing around and putting things in boxes
thinking about something else

5 **Text Evidence:** "Ahmed and his family also are moving to the city, and we will be neighbors."

UNIT 1 WEEK 3

Item #	Content Focus
1	Cause and Effect
2	Vocabulary: Context Clues
3	Cause and Effect
4	Vocabulary: Context Clues
5	Cause and Effect

Suggested Responses:

1. **Text Evidence:** along the sand dunes near San Francisco; the sand and waves Adams learned to find peace in nature.

2. **Text Evidence:** steep

3. **Text Evidence:** Later, Adams worked for the Sierra Club; The job was at Yosemite.

4. **Text Evidence:** amazed by what he saw
   amazing or wonderful

5. They saw the photos that Adams took at Yosemite.
   Text Evidence: People in Congress saw his pictures, too. As a result, they created more national parks like Yosemite.

UNIT 1 WEEK 4

Item #	Content Focus
1	Sequence
2	Sequence
3	Vocabulary: Context Clues
4	Sequence
5	Vocabulary: Context Clues

Suggested Responses:

1. Ray made a computer that wrote music. It won first prize in a science fair.
   Text Evidence: in the 1960s

2. **Text Evidence:** In the 1970s; As they talked

3. **Text Evidence:** a scanner; a computer music keyboard
   machines or tools

4. Ray invented a machine that could make the sounds of any instrument.

5. **Text Evidence:** eagerly supported
   to do something with great excitement

UNIT 1 WEEK 5

Item #	Content Focus
1	Vocabulary: Context Clues
2	Author's Point of View
3	Vocabulary: Context Clues
4	Author's Point of View
5	Author's Point of View

Suggested Responses:

1. **Text Evidence:** a close look

2. **Text Evidence:** E-books have great features; E-books are easy to carry around.
   Benefits of E-Books

3. **Text Evidence:** problems

4. The author thinks it can be a big problem.
   Text Evidence: If you forget to charge it, you cannot read the book.

5. E-books are a better choice than books printed on paper.
   Text Evidence: With all of the benefits that e-books have, they are the clear winner!

UNIT 2 WEEK 1

Item #	Content Focus
1	Problem and Solution
2	Vocabulary: Context Clues
3	Problem and Solution
4	Vocabulary: Context Clues
5	Problem and Solution

Suggested Responses:

1. The country needed a new government and a new leader.
   Text Evidence: [A box should be drawn around the entire section titled "The Great Debate."]

2. **Text Evidence:** this meeting
   a meeting for a special purpose

3. **Text Evidence:** Others thought a king might have too much power. He could not be fired, and no one would have a say in choosing future kings.

4. **Text Evidence:** How would the new leader be chosen? How much power would he have?
   to talk about or discuss something

5. The Constitution explained the U.S. President's job and what he could do and could not do. It solved the problem of how the new leader should run the country.

UNIT 2 WEEK 2

Item #	Content Focus
1	Compare and Contrast
2	Vocabulary: Context Clues
3	Compare and Contrast
4	Vocabulary: Context Clues
5	Compare and Contrast

Suggested Responses:

1 **Text Evidence:** Once, there was a village with two excellent bakers.
One baker is jolly and gives children treats. The other baker is unkind and does not give children treats.

2 **Text Evidence:** the name of the new royal baker
announce or make something known

3 **Text Evidence:** "My chocolate cake will win," he said. "It is the best in the land!"
Possible answer: The jolly baker is not as confident as the unkind baker.

4 **Text Evidence:** did not know

5 The unkind baker puffs out his chest with pride. The jolly baker smiles at Polly and whispers, "Lemon!"

UNIT 2 WEEK 3

Item #	Content Focus
1	Sequence
2	Sequence
3	Vocabulary: Context Clues
4	Vocabulary: Context Clues
5	Sequence

Suggested Responses:

1 **Text Evidence:** 1849
22 years later

2 **Text Evidence:** He created a new type of potato in 1871 that is still the most used potato today.
Burbank sold the rights to the potato for $150 and then moved to California.

3 **Text Evidence:** active

4 **Text Evidence:** grew a cactus that had no spines, or needles
changed or made different

5 Possible answer: Burbank used new ways to create and grow more than 800 new types of plants.
Text Evidence: 1926

UNIT 2 WEEK 4

Item #	Content Focus
1	Theme
2	Vocabulary: Context Clues
3	Theme
4	Vocabulary: Context Clues
5	Theme

Suggested Responses:

1 He wants the other animals to respect him.

2 **Text Evidence:** thanks

3 **Text Evidence:** He decided that he would capture Snake, one of the longest, strongest animals in the forest.
Possible answer: Anansi is brave and clever.

4 **Text Evidence:** with the hope of catching him
chase

5 **Text Evidence:** From that day on, the animals treated Anansi with respect.
Possible answer: You do not have to be big and strong to gain respect from others.

UNIT 2 WEEK 5

Item #	Content Focus
1	Genre
2	Literary Elements: Rhyme
3	Literary Elements: Repetition
4	Theme
5	Theme

Suggested Responses:

1 **Text Evidence:** "Let's help!" I say to classmates. / "Let's make a plan today. / We'll plan to have a car wash. / And hold it Saturday!"
The dialogue helps to tell a story about what the speaker does.

2 today/Saturday

3 **Text Evidence:** To kids in Africa; in America
Possible answer: Kids in America can help kids in Africa.

4 **Text Evidence:** A desk can make a difference—; "We'll plan to have a car wash."; We earn some cash to send desks—

5 The speaker helps kids in Africa by raising money to send desks to them.

UNIT 3 WEEK 1

Item #	Content Focus
1	Theme
2	Vocabulary: Context Clues
3	Theme
4	Vocabulary: Context Clues
5	Theme

Suggested Responses:

1. upset and embarrassed
   Text Evidence: Cara frowned; Cara never understood why he wore those odd clothes.

2. **Text Evidence:** Without thinking
   said something suddenly without thinking

3. **Text Evidence:** "I really like that my grandmother is different from everyone else."

4. **Text Evidence:** embarrassment
   thankful and proud

5. Cara learns to respect and admire what makes her family different.

UNIT 3 WEEK 2

Item #	Content Focus
1	Vocabulary: Context Clues
2	Theme
3	Vocabulary: Context Clues
4	Theme
5	Theme

Suggested Responses:

1. **Text Evidence:** way of life
   the way a group of people live in one place over a period of time

2. **Text Evidence:** "Help me gather grasses and reeds along the river." Adam had learned that ancient Egyptians used these plants to build.
   Adam and his dad use them to build a hut for shelter.

3. **Text Evidence:** a hut made from mud and reeds
   made or built

4. **Text Evidence:** "You have used our resources well," the boy said. "I will share a secret."

5. Possible answer: Adam and his dad are able to build a shelter in an unfamiliar place because of their knowledge.

UNIT 3 WEEK 3

Item #	Content Focus
1	Vocabulary: Context Clues
2	Main Idea and Key Details
3	Vocabulary: Context Clues
4	Main Idea and Key Details
5	Main Idea and Key Details

Suggested Responses:

1 **Text Evidence:** a pattern again and again
something that happens again and again

2 **Text Evidence:** in many objects, such as pinecones and seashells.

3 **Text Evidence:** if you look at a sunflower
able to be seen

4 **Text Evidence:** Add the last two numbers each time to find the next number in the pattern.
13 (8 + 5)

5 Possible answer: Leonardo Fibonacci discovered a mathematical pattern that is often found in nature.

UNIT 3 WEEK 4

Item #	Content Focus
1	Main Idea and Key Details
2	Vocabulary: Context Clues
3	Vocabulary: Context Clues
4	Main Idea and Key Details
5	Main Idea and Key Details

Suggested Responses:

1 **Text Evidence:** Around the world, many people do not have medicines they need. In some places, women have few rights. Often, people work long hours in difficult conditions, making very little money.

2 **Text Evidence:** their time and effort
given or devoted

3 **Text Evidence:** working together closely
work together to do something

4 **Text Evidence:** They interview people, take pictures, and write articles as ways of sharing their discoveries.
Some groups learn about the problems and donate money.

5 **Text Evidence:** She traveled to Africa with Nick. They made a movie about poverty and disease there.
Nick's student partners help the world learn about problems that others face.

UNIT 3 WEEK 5

Item #	Content Focus
1	Author's Point of View
2	Vocabulary: Context Clues
3	Author's Point of View
4	Vocabulary: Context Clues
5	Author's Point of View

Suggested Responses:

1 Possible answer: The author is impressed by the moai.
Text Evidence: incredible

2 **Text Evidence:** hundreds of years ago; people did not have animals or wheels
a period of time or history

3 Possible answer: All of the measurements show that the moai were very large, or gigantic.

4 **Text Evidence:** These pieces showed

5 **Text Evidence:** they rocked a statue side to side with ropes, and it slowly moved forward.
This method needed just 18 people, which is not many at all.

UNIT 4 WEEK 1

Item #	Content Focus
1	Point of View
2	Point of View
3	Vocabulary: Context Clues
4	Point of View
5	Vocabulary: Context Clues

Suggested Responses:

1 **Text Evidence:** she; her

2 **Text Evidence:** born in Missouri; looked just like a regular girl; could ride a horse before
she could even talk; more than six feet tall; tamed wild broncos and hunted better than
any man on this side of the Mississippi; joined the army.
The detail about Calamity Jane riding a horse before she could talk is probably not true.

3 **Text Evidence:** missions; act
acts or actions

4 The narrator thinks Calamity Jane is very courageous.
Text Evidence: One act of courage

5 **Text Evidence:** acts of bravery
brave and courageous

UNIT 4 WEEK 2

Item #	Content Focus
1	Point of View
2	Vocabulary: Context Clues
3	Point of View
4	Vocabulary: Context Clues
5	Point of View

Suggested Responses:

1. **Text Evidence:** Jada

2. **Text Evidence:** I can't find any of my soccer collection anywhere.
   confused and upset

3. **Text Evidence:** *(Looking doubtful and mumbling to herself)*
   doubtful

4. **Text Evidence:** *She looks in JON'S room and sees a scrapbook, glue, and one of her photos;* Jon is definitely up to something!
   doubtful or unsure about something; questioning the truth of something

5. She is happy that Jon put her soccer collection in a scrapbook.
   Text Evidence: *(Relieved and excited);* This is the best birthday present ever!

UNIT 4 WEEK 3

Item #	Content Focus
1	Vocabulary: Context Clues
2	Author's Point of View
3	Author's Point of View
4	Vocabulary: Context Clues
5	Author's Point of View

Suggested Responses:

1. **Text Evidence:** laws that were not fair

2. **Text Evidence:** Coretta worked with her husband to peacefully fight for equal rights. Together, they helped to get the Civil Rights Act passed in 1964.
   The author probably agrees with Coretta that equal rights were important to fight for.

3. The author feels that Martin Luther King, Jr. had a big influence on people's rights and that he made a positive change around the world.

4. **Text Evidence:** She spoke openly about social issues and wrote a newspaper column.
   tending to speak openly and directly

5. **Text Evidence:** Her work still inspires many people today.
   The author thinks that Coretta accomplished many positive things in her lifetime and that she is still an inspiration to people today.

UNIT 4 WEEK 4

Item #	Content Focus
1	Author's Point of View
2	Vocabulary: Context Clues
3	Author's Point of View
4	Vocabulary: Context Clues
5	Author's Point of View

Suggested Responses:

1. Possible answer: The author believes that wind is a good source of energy.
Text Evidence: For centuries, people have depended on wind energy to meet their needs.

2. **Text Evidence:** there was not a lot of oil available in the U.S. People counted on oil as a source of energy
something that is required or needed

3. Wind farms are now being built in oceans because of the strong breezes there; There are no buildings or trees to block the wind.

4. **Text Evidence:** protect

5. The chart shows that most of the energy that the U.S. uses comes from coal, and coal will eventually run out.

UNIT 4 WEEK 5

Item #	Content Focus
1	Genre
2	Theme
3	Literary Elements: Stanza
4	Literary Elements: Alliteration
5	Theme

Suggested Responses:

1. The poem shows the speaker's ideas and feelings and does not rhyme.

2. **Text Evidence:** I am joined to my skateboard; my board is part of me. / We are one…halves of each other…the same.

3. **Text Evidence:** I am soulful and serious / Falling…flying…free!
The speaker enjoys skateboarding and feels free while he is doing it.

4. **Text Evidence:** Twisting and turning, stretching and straining.
The speaker describes the way his body moves while he skateboards.

5. Possible answer: Skateboarding can be an important expression of self.

UNIT 5 WEEK 1

Item #	Content Focus
1	Compare and Contrast
2	Vocabulary: Context Clues
3	Compare and Contrast
4	Vocabulary: Context Clues
5	Compare and Contrast

Suggested Responses:

1. **Text Evidence:** "I wish I could play hockey like you do. Do you think you could show me how to pass and shoot on the ice today?"

2. **Text Evidence:** Paying attention to hockey
concentrating or paying attention to something

3. **Text Evidence:** But it was too late, and Tom shrugged and mumbled, "Thanks, but George and I have been working together on it; Tom shrugged and said, "Maybe."
Tom is now disappointed with Sanjay for not wanting to skate with him.

4. **Text Evidence:** better than anyone they had ever seen
Excellent

5. **Text Evidence:** "I may be a great skater," thought Sanjay, "but I have something new to practice—being a much better friend."
Sanjay will focus more on his friendships than on himself.

UNIT 5 WEEK 2

Item #	Content Focus
1	Compare and Contrast
2	Vocabulary: Context Clues
3	Vocabulary: Context Clues
4	Compare and Contrast
5	Compare and Contrast

Suggested Responses:

1. Emily and the other girls have difficult work conditions at the Lowell Mill.

2. **Text Evidence:** Emily's shoulders ached; she did not stop working
someone who is weak in some way

3. **Text Evidence:** The other girls would not take pity on her as they, too, worked hard.
feelings of support for someone

4. Clara does not think that any change will happen if the girls refuse to work.

5. **Text Evidence:** Emily smiled; Already, her shoulders felt better.
At the end of the passage, she has a better view towards work.

Weekly Assessment · Answer Key

UNIT 5 WEEK 3

Item #	Content Focus
1	Compare and Contrast
2	Vocabulary: Context Clues
3	Compare and Contrast
4	Vocabulary: Context Clues
5	Compare and Contrast

Suggested Responses:

1. **Text Evidence:** Scientists have worried about saving whales for years
protecting whales' hearing

2. **Text Evidence:** much more noise pollution
in a way that deserves attention

3. In the past, the noises were from nature. Today, they are louder and come from manmade activities.

4. **Text Evidence:** Loud noises impact their hearing and affect their ability to use it.
has an effect on

5. **Text Evidence:** Military sonar

UNIT 5 WEEK 4

Item #	Content Focus
1	Cause and Effect
2	Cause and Effect
3	Vocabulary: Context Clues
4	Vocabulary: Context Clues
5	Cause and Effect

Suggested Responses:

1. **Text Evidence:** one day an apple dropped on Sir Isaac Newton's head

2. **Text Evidence:** the university closed for several years
He learned about the universe and how it works.

3. **Text Evidence:** the movement of objects in outer space
related to astronomy, the study of objects in outer space

4. go around

5. It will cause the ball to fall back to the ground.

UNIT 5 WEEK 5

Item #	Content Focus
1	Author's Point of View
2	Vocabulary: Context Clues
3	Author's Point of View
4	Vocabulary: Context Clues
5	Author's Point of View

Suggested Responses:

1 **Text Evidence:** Each U.S. family owns about 25 electronics. We only recycle about 14% of these, so most are thrown away in landfills.
We create a lot of e-waste because we own so many electronics and recycle so few.

2 **Text Evidence:** around the world
happening over a large area or affecting many people

3 **Text Evidence:** As workers take apart these machines, unsafe chemicals are released into the air.

4 **Text Evidence:** soil and crops
having to do with farms or farming

5 The chart shows that we do not recycle enough electronics and that there will be much more e-waste in the future.
Text Evidence: More laws are needed to make sure electronics are recycled safely. People should also think carefully before buying the next new product.

UNIT 6 WEEK 1

Item #	Content Focus
1	Theme
2	Vocabulary: Context Clues
3	Theme
4	Vocabulary: Context Clues
5	Theme

Suggested Responses:

1 **Text Evidence:** I took these words to heart.
The narrator is motivated by these words to join the Peace Corps.

2 **Text Evidence:** we help to educate children in Ghana
ways of helping or giving services without payment

3 They felt that they could help the people of Ghana.

4 **Text Evidence:** learning about African culture, how to manage a classroom, and getting kids excited about learning
new members of a group or organization

5 **Text Evidence:** My work is difficult, but completely worth it. I will always remember my time here and the people I helped along the way.

UNIT 6 WEEK 2

Item #	Content Focus
1	Vocabulary: Context Clues
2	Theme
3	Theme
4	Vocabulary: Context Clues
5	Theme

Suggested Responses:

1. **Text Evidence:** helmet
   something that helps to keep you safe

2. **Text Evidence:** Randy thought about keeping the basketball

3. **Text Evidence:** he knew it was his responsibility to find the owner
   Derrick is relieved and happy to have his ball back.

4. **Text Evidence:** Throughout the day, he asked other students who might own it. Their responses made Randy feel confident that the ball belonged to Derrick.
   certain or sure

5. It is important to do the right thing and return what does not belong to you.

UNIT 6 WEEK 3

Item #	Content Focus
1	Vocabulary: Context Clues
2	Cause and Effect
3	Cause and Effect
4	Cause and Effect
5	Vocabulary: Context Clues

Suggested Responses:

1. **Text Evidencee:** Animals go through physical changes to survive in their environment.

2. **Text Evidence:** It has huge eyes that can see very well at night when it hunts for food.
   Their heads can turn around to spot prey from almost any direction.

3. **Text Evidence:** The pupil in a cat's eye can expand to a large circle to allow more light inside.
   The cat is able to more easily hunt for prey at night.

4. It helps them view a wider area at once and avoid attacks by predators.

5. **Text Evidence:** look for food on the ground
   search for food

UNIT 6 WEEK 4

Item #	Content Focus
1	Problem and Solution
2	Vocabulary: Context Clues
3	Problem and Solution
4	Vocabulary: Context Clues
5	Problem and Solution

Suggested Responses:

1. **Text Evidence:** natural resources are limited and rules must be put in place before these resources run out

2. **Text Evidence:** asking them to save our lands
asked or strongly recommended

3. **Text Evidences:** Between 1901 and 1909, Roosevelt took action to protect almost 230 million acres of land; Roosevelt also signed the National Monuments Act; the creation of five national parks, the country's first 18 national monuments, and 150 national forests; He started 21 projects that helped to renew land so it would become useful again.

4. **Text Evidence:** the Grand Canyon
a view of scenery or land

5. Possible answer: Roosevelt protected natural resources that are still important today.
Text Evidence: Some of Roosevelt's greatest achievements were in helping our planet. Many people remember him as the country's environmental President.

UNIT 6 WEEK 5

Item #	Content Focus
1	Point of View
2	Literary Elements: Assonance
3	Genre
4	Point of View
5	Point of View

Suggested Responses:

1. **Text Evidence:** I shed a few tears; "When will I see you again?"; "That's just not the same!" I wailed.

2. **Text Evidence:** we e-mail each week; she greets me

3. The speaker uses characters, dialogue, and imagery to tell a story.

4. **Text Evidence:** I'm learning new expressions—my favorite is "Ni chi fan le ma? "Have you eaten rice yet?"

5. The speaker likes being e-pen pals with Pang and learning about her culture.
Text Evidence: Being e-pen pals isn't so bad. We stay connected halfway across the world—two friends, two cultures to share!

Mid-Unit Assessment Answer Key

UNIT 1

Item #	Answer	Content Focus
1	B	Vocabulary: Context Clues
2	B	Problem and Solution
3	C	Problem and Solution
4	B	Sequence
5	A	Sequence
6	B	Cause and Effect
7	C	Cause and Effect
8	A	Vocabulary: Context Clues
9	B	Text Features: Primary Source
10	B	Vocabulary: Context Clues

UNIT 2

Item #	Answer	Content Focus
1	B	Vocabulary: Context Clues
2	A	Compare and Contrast
3	C	Vocabulary: Context Clues
4	B	Compare and Contrast
5	B	Vocabulary: Context Clues
6	A	Sequence
7	C	Sequence
8	B	Problem and Solution
9	C	Problem and Solution
10	C	Text Features: Time Line

UNIT 3

Item #	Answer	Content Focus
1	B	Vocabulary: Context Clues
2	A	Theme
3	C	Vocabulary: Context Clues
4	C	Theme
5	A	Theme
6	C	Vocabulary: Context Clues
7	C	Main Idea and Key Details
8	B	Main Idea and Key Details
9	A	Main Idea and Key Details
10	A	Text Features: Diagram

UNIT 4

Item #	Answer	Content Focus
1	A	Point of View
2	A	Point of View
3	C	Vocabulary: Context Clues
4	C	Point of View
5	B	Vocabulary: Context Clues
6	B	Author's Point of View
7	B	Vocabulary: Context Clues
8	C	Author's Point of View
9	B	Author's Point of View
10	A	Author's Point of View

UNIT 5

Item #	Answer	Content Focus
1	B	Vocabulary: Context Clues
2	B	Compare and Contrast
3	C	Compare and Contrast
4	A	Vocabulary: Context Clues
5	C	Compare and Contrast
6	C	Compare and Contrast
7	A	Vocabulary: Context Clues
8	B	Compare and Contrast
9	B	Compare and Contrast
10	A	Text Features: Graph

UNIT 6

Item #	Answer	Content Focus
1	C	Vocabulary: Context Clues
2	A	Theme
3	B	Vocabulary: Context Clues
4	B	Theme
5	A	Theme
6	C	Cause and Effect
7	B	Vocabulary: Context Clues
8	A	Cause and Effect
9	C	Cause and Effect
10	A	Text Features: Map

Mid-Unit Assessment · Answer Key

Unit Assessment Answer Key

UNIT 1

Item #	Answer	Content Focus
1	C	Problem and Solution
2	A	Sequence
3	C	Vocabulary: Context Clues
4	A	Problem and Solution
5	B	Vocabulary: Context Clues
6	B	Vocabulary: Context Clues
7	C	Sequence
8	A	Cause and Effect
9	B	Cause and Effect
10	B	Vocabulary: Context Clues
11	A	Author's Point of View
12	C	Text Features: Headings
13	A	Cause and Effect
14	A	Vocabulary: Context Clues
15	C	Author's Point of View

UNIT 2

Item #	Answer	Content Focus
1	B	Theme
2	B	Compare and Contrast
3	A	Vocabulary: Context Clues
4	C	Compare and Contrast
5	B	Vocabulary: Context Clues
6	A	Compare and Contrast
7	B	Vocabulary: Context Clues
8	A	Theme
9	B	Problem and Solution
10	B	Sequence
11	A	Sequence
12	C	Vocabulary: Context Clues
13	A	Problem and Solution
14	C	Vocabulary: Context Clues
15	B	Text Features: Time Line

Unit Assessment · Answer Key

UNIT 3

Item #	Answer	Content Focus
1	A	Vocabulary: Context Clues
2	C	Theme
3	C	Theme
4	B	Theme
5	A	Theme
6	B	Vocabulary: Context Clues
7	C	Theme
8	A	Author's Point of View
9	A	Vocabulary: Context Clues
10	C	Vocabulary: Context Clues
11	B	Author's Point of View
12	C	Vocabulary: Context Clues
13	A	Main Idea and Key Details
14	C	Main Idea and Key Details
15	A	Text Features: Diagram

UNIT 4

Item #	Answer	Content Focus
1	C	Point of View
2	A	Vocabulary: Context Clues
3	B	Point of View
4	B	Theme
5	C	Theme
6	B	Vocabulary: Context Clues
7	A	Point of View
8	C	Author's Point of View
9	C	Vocabulary: Context Clues
10	A	Author's Point of View
11	A	Author's Point of View
12	B	Vocabulary: Context Clues
13	B	Vocabulary: Context Clues
14	A	Author's Point of View
15	C	Text Features: Chart

Unit Assessment · Answer Key

UNIT 5

Item #	Answer	Content Focus
1	A	Compare and Contrast
2	A	Vocabulary: Context Clues
3	B	Compare and Contrast
4	A	Compare and Contrast
5	B	Vocabulary: Context Clues
6	B	Vocabulary: Context Clues
7	C	Compare and Contrast
8	B	Vocabulary: Context Clues
9	A	Cause and Effect
10	B	Compare and Contrast
11	C	Vocabulary: Context Clues
12	B	Author's Point of View
13	C	Cause and Effect
14	A	Author's Point of View
15	A	Text Features: Graph

UNIT 6

Item #	Answer	Content Focus
1	B	Vocabulary: Context Clues
2	A	Point of View
3	A	Theme
4	B	Vocabulary: Context Clues
5	B	Vocabulary: Context Clues
6	C	Point of View
7	A	Theme
8	B	Cause and Effect
9	A	Cause and Effect
10	B	Vocabulary: Context Clues
11	B	Problem and Solution
12	C	Problem and Solution
13	B	Vocabulary: Context Clues
14	A	Problem and Solution
15	B	Text Features: Map

Unit Assessment · Answer Key

Exit Assessment Answer Key

UNIT 1

Item #	Answer	Content Focus
1	C	Vocabulary: Context Clues
2	A	Problem and Solution
3	B	Vocabulary: Context Clues
4	B	Sequence
5	C	Problem and Solution
6	A	Vocabulary: Context Clues
7	B	Sequence
8	A	Vocabulary: Context Clues
9	C	Cause and Effect
10	A	Cause and Effect
11	C	Author's Point of View
12	B	Vocabulary: Context Clues
13	A	Cause and Effect
14	C	Author's Point of View
15	A	Text Features: Primary Source

UNIT 2

Item #	Answer	Content Focus
1	C	Vocabulary: Context Clues
2	A	Sequence
3	B	Vocabulary: Context Clues
4	C	Problem and Solution
5	C	Vocabulary: Context Clues
6	A	Sequence
7	B	Problem and Solution
8	B	Text Features: Time Line
9	A	Vocabulary: Context Clues
10	A	Theme
11	C	Compare and Contrast
12	A	Theme
13	A	Vocabulary: Context Clues
14	C	Theme
15	B	Compare and Contrast

UNIT 3

Item #	Answer	Content Focus
1	C	Theme
2	B	Theme
3	B	Theme
4	A	Vocabulary: Context Clues
5	C	Theme
6	C	Theme
7	B	Vocabulary: Context Clues
8	A	Author's Point of View
9	A	Vocabulary: Context Clues
10	C	Main Idea and Key Details
11	B	Author's Point of View
12	B	Vocabulary: Context Clues
13	C	Main Idea and Key Details
14	B	Vocabulary: Context Clues
15	A	Text Features: Diagram

UNIT 4

Item #	Answer	Content Focus
1	A	Point of View
2	A	Point of View
3	C	Theme
4	C	Vocabulary: Context Clues
5	B	Theme
6	A	Vocabulary: Context Clues
7	C	Theme
8	C	Author's Point of View
9	B	Vocabulary: Context Clues
10	B	Author's Point of View
11	A	Vocabulary: Context Clues
12	C	Author's Point of View
13	A	Vocabulary: Context Clues
14	A	Author's Point of View
15	C	Text Features: Chart

Exit Assessment · Answer Key

UNIT 5

Item #	Answer	Content Focus
1	B	Compare and Contrast
2	A	Vocabulary: Context Clues
3	A	Vocabulary: Context Clues
4	C	Compare and Contrast
5	B	Compare and Contrast
6	C	Vocabulary: Context Clues
7	A	Compare and Contrast
8	C	Author's Point of View
9	A	Cause and Effect
10	B	Cause and Effect
11	B	Vocabulary: Context Clues
12	A	Compare and Contrast
13	A	Vocabulary: Context Clues
14	C	Author's Point of View
15	B	Text Features: Graph

UNIT 6

Item #	Answer	Content Focus
1	C	Point of View
2	B	Point of View
3	B	Vocabulary: Context Clues
4	C	Theme
5	A	Vocabulary: Context Clues
6	B	Vocabulary: Context Clues
7	C	Theme
8	B	Vocabulary: Context Clues
9	B	Cause and Effect
10	C	Problem and Solution
11	C	Cause and Effect
12	B	Vocabulary: Context Clues
13	B	Cause and Effect
14	A	Problem and Solution
15	C	Text Features: Map

Exit Assessment • Answer Key